KITT
PEAK

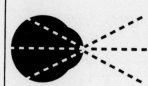

KITT PEAK

AN EVANS NOVEL OF THE WEST

AL SARRANTONIO

Thorndike Press • Thorndike, Maine

Thorndike Large Print ® Popular Series edition published in 1993 by arrangement with M. Evans & Co., Inc.

The tree indicium in a trademark of Thorndike Press.

Set in 16 pt. News Plantin by Ginny Beaulieu.

This book is printed on acid-free, high opacity paper. ∞

Library of Congress Cataloging in Publication Data

Sarrantonio, Al.
    Kitt Peak / Al Sarrantonio.
      p. cm.
    ISBN 1-56054-773-1 (alk. paper : lg. print)
    1. Large type books. I. Title.
  [PS3569.A73K57 1993b]
  813'.54—dc20
                                 93-8262
                                    CIP

For
Pat LoBrutto
Who's been there

Chapter One

Bad day.

They had all been bad days lately. Thomas thought about other times when there had been no bad days, only days to get work done, to work with his hands and mind. Even when bad things were involved — even when death was involved — his days in the Army, as the very first Negro lieutenant in the Buffalo Soldiers, the all-Negro regiment of the cavalry, had been good ones.

Foolishness, he thought.

Steel your mind.

It seemed as if he had spent a lot of time lately steeling his mind. And it seemed as if it was getting harder to do. Retirement did not agree with him; and even the Sherlock Holmes stories, which had always brought him so much joy, and which he still looked forward to receiving every six months in a packet of *Strand* magazines sent from New York, brought him little solace these days. It was as if his restless mind could no longer concentrate on mere fiction, that the loss of his vocation had, over the last months, begun to turn him into the one thing he had always guarded against.

You're soft, Thomas.

You're soft and if you don't watch it, you're going to get old.

He rose from the chair he had been sitting in, the one facing the front window of his home on Maple Street in Boston, Massachusetts, and waved an impatient hand at the air.

Bah, he thought, *it's all foolishness. I'm already soft, and already old. An old man sitting in front of the window waiting for the mail.*

Out of the corner of his eye he caught movement on the street outside, and turned to face the window again. Sure enough, the mailman was making his slow way up the path toward the house. John Reynolds, his name was. Bundled up to the chin against the cold, with his cap pulled down over his earmuffs. He looked like a blue tick.

The mailman caught his eye through the frosted window, and Thomas started to wave his hand in greeting; but Reynolds merely looked away, scowling. Another bigot in a country of bigots. Thomas was sure that if the force of the federal government wasn't behind Reynolds, the man would have dropped the mail in the snow and walked away.

As it was, there was the sound of the mailman jamming the letters into the box and hurrying away, his back to Thomas as he left the gate open on his way to the next house.

Scowling himself, biting back his anger, Thomas went to the door, opened it, bracing himself against the blast of cold air that pushed in, pulled the crumpled mail from its wall box, and closed the door again.

His pension check was not among the creased letters, and, momentarily, another flare of anger rose and then died within him. *Damned bureaucrats.* Ever since Roosevelt had come to office in 1901, two years ago, the system of government had come to a complete halt. The damned Republican cared more about trees and bears than he did about the men who had fought, and too often died, in Indian wars, making the West safe for white settlers. And Roosevelt of all people, who had at least been out there himself, seen the land with his own eyes, experienced at least some of the hardships, and knew what it was like . . .

A single letter fell from the mass of handbills and fluttered to the floor. For a moment hope rose within Thomas, thinking that maybe the check had come at last. For an instant, he even thought that perhaps Roosevelt wasn't a bad sort after all —

But it was not a government check at all. Thomas raised the envelope to the lighted window. There was something dimly familiar about the scrawl of handwriting on the face. The letter looked as though it had been through a war. Besides the mailman's crumpling, the letter was torn in one corner and stained with something that looked like coffee across the front. The lettering on the address was smudged.

Thomas turned the letter directly to the light. The coffee stain, up close, was clotted and uneven. . . .

Chicory coffee.

Only chicory coffee would leave that distinctive gritty blotch. And the handwriting . . .

The lettering, he now saw, was not smudged at all, but had been written with a dipped quill in a trembling hand. A blotter had been badly employed, further running the letters. The writing *was* familiar. . . .

Adams. Bill Adams, one of the very few white men in the 101st Cavalry worth a spit. He had been Thomas's friend and confidant, the only nonprivate, with the exception of young Sergeant Chase, who had been sorry to see Thomas retire.

But Adams had never trembled over anything, not at Fraser Pass during the war with Victorio, not in the teeth of death in Limpia Canyon, when surrounded by an overwhelming force of rogue Mescaleros commanded by Victorio's vengeance-seeking brother. . . .

Thomas almost tore the letter open, then hesitated over the tear along one edge.

Examining it more closely, he saw that the tear had been made deliberately, a small thumb-ripped opening that had then been straightened down the edge by the pull of a knife or letter opener. But the would-be opener had hesitated before the letter could be pulled out, and had abandoned his task.

Thomas faced the letter toward the window again, and studied the postmark.

April 14, 1902.

Nine months ago.

And with a postmark from Tucson, Arizona.

Is that where Adams was?

Again suppressing an urge to open the letter, Thomas instead crossed the room, lay the letter down on a lamp table while he bent to pull a wooden cartridge box from under his bed. He had to move aside a stack of *Strand* magazines to get at the box, which was covered with dust. He rested the box on his knees and blew the dust off. Glancing at the unmade covers of the bed, he winced momentarily, realizing just how soft he had become. Instead of sharp military corners, the covers were piled in a heap, unmade.

He thought of Sherlock Holmes.

At least I haven't reduced myself to taking cocaine.

He shook his head.

That's no excuse.

He turned his attention to the box, and went slowly through it. Two letters from Lincoln Reeves on top, the most recent received nearly a month before. Whose turn was it to write? With shame, he realized that he had not written back to Reeves, not answered either this letter or the last. The young man he had thought of as his Watson must wonder at this point if Thomas was even alive.

He set the two letters aside on the unmade bed, resolving to answer them this day.

Next were family papers, the deed for this very house from his deceased Aunt Martha Johnston Mullin. The house had been left to her by the abolitionist Fay Gordon, who had died proud though nearly penniless after Boston ostracized her for her relationship with a former black slave. There were other papers relating to the property, various town ordinances meant to ostracize the property itself, abolitionist lawyer writs blocking those moves by the city of Boston, etc.

Next was a flat of cardboard, and beneath that, Thomas's Army papers.

He had located the last correspondence from

Bill Adams in a moment. Nearly three years. The handwriting on the last letter, from Adams's newest, and last, post at Fort Brayden, in northern Arizona, was firm and confident. He remembered the letter as being full of hope. Adams would be retiring in six months, and moving to Arizona to live with his daughter. There had been some chatting about old times, about how they would have to get together after Adams's retirement even though both of them knew that would probably not happen, about Bill's sorrow that Thomas's bid for reenlistment had been turned down. Thomas even recalled Adam's phrasing, "They stepped on your neck real good, Thomas, and I'm sorry there's nothing I can do about it. Comes with the territory of laying low on the ladder all these years. If only Grierson or one of the other mucky-mucks were still in power in Washington . . ."

Thomas lay the letter back in the cartridge box, rose, and retrieved Adams's new letter from the lamp table.

So . . . he thought, a faint stirring of juices long dormant, of interest and excitement, already beginning to rise within him.

He opened the letter carefully, unsticking the back flap, noting how carelessly it had been sealed to begin with.

13

He pulled the letter from within.

As he unfolded and looked at it, a pang of sorrow drowned out the rise of interest; but then the excitement quickly overcame the sorrow, pushing it to the back of his mind.

He pulled the letter up to his nose. It nearly reeked of alcohol. An amber stain, different from the coffee stain on the envelope, washed the upper right-hand corner of the page. That was where Adams would have kept his whiskey glass. He was, Thomas remembered, right-handed. And so, that coffee stain on the envelope was evidence that the letter had been written in the throes of alcohol, and was probably sealed and mailed during the aftermath of attempted recovery, while Adams had been drinking coffee.

The letter was dated April 10th, bearing this out.

If anything, the handwriting on the letter was even worse than that on the envelope.

Thomas folded the letter flat on the table top and read:

Dear Thomas,

It is not with joy that I write you this time, I'm afraid. Things have not gone as I had planned. Perhaps if this were the Army, things could be handled differently, but I doubt it. We both know how the Army operates, and in this case the result would be no better. There is a man in Tempe, name of Cross, who would help, but I heard he's out with the 66th, scouting, and won't be back from California for at least eighteen months. He owes me, but that's another story.

My Abby is gone, Thomas. . . .

Here there was an obvious pause while Adams took a drink; there was evidence that the spill on the letter had occurred at this point. Thomas could almost see his friend blotting the alcohol from the page before continuing. The letter went on:

I'll be honest with you, because you'd figure out anyway that I'm in the bottle and feeling badly. Seems I invested a bit too much in my life after the Army, and when things did not turn out as I planned I took a bit of a fall.

But my Abby, as I said, is gone. She's only nineteen, now, Thomas, you may remember my talking about her years ago. To me she was only a baby then, and her momma was raising her on the Papagos reservation here, though in Christian ways. In my head, she was always my little girl, but when I came back to Tucson she was all grown up, with ideas of her own. She didn't want to live in Tucson City with me, at least not at first; but even after she came to live with me I could see she wasn't happy. But then, things seemed to get better. And then she disappeared.

Again there was a pause, Thomas could feel it. And once again when the man went back to writing, he was drunker, and his hand less steady:

Thomas, I'm a desperate man, if you can't tell. Abby's mother was a good woman, and tried to raise her the way I wanted.

I have no right to ask this of you, old friend. I realize that Boston must seem very far away from the Army and from Arizona, but . . .

Again a lengthy pause, before Adams asked the question he felt he had to steal himself to ask:

You're the best friend I've ever known, Thomas, and the best tracker. If you could help me, I would be beholden to you for my life. I hesitate to ask you for old times' sake, but if that's all that it takes, for my daughter, I'll do that. All right, my daughter is

16

Injun, at least half, but she's all I have, and I don't want a horrible thing to happen. I'm afraid I must sign off now with this plea I've made. . . .

The letter was unsigned, with a running line, blotted carelessly, after the last word. Perhaps Adams had thought to reopen the letter, remembering that he hadn't signed it. Thomas wondered, also, if the man had hesitated to ask for his help, or found it so difficult, because Thomas was Negro.
That's an evil thought.
Sighing, Thomas walked to the window and looked out. Still holding the letter, he put his hands behind his back and clasped them. No, it wasn't such an evil thought. As much as Bill Adams was a friend, he had still found it difficult to ask Thomas's help, simply because of the difference in their skin color. Adams would deny it, but still, here in this time, thirty years after the War Between the States, Thomas was a second-class citizen merely because his skin was dark. In the Army, especially in the Buffalo Soldiers, the difference between him and Adams had been easier to ignore; but here, in the real world, the stigma was unavoidable.
Thomas stared out at the January white of

Boston, where the people professed equality but didn't live it, and thought of the warmness of Tucson.

Adams had found it difficult to ask.

But he *had* asked.

I'll help you, old friend, Thomas thought. *I'll help you merely because you're my friend, and, almost as importantly, because if I don't, if I stay here in two-faced Boston, pacing the rooms of this little house and brooding, I will lose my mind, along with the rest of my pride.*

Having decided, Thomas turned away from the window. There was a perceptible smile on his face. He held the letter almost lovingly in his hand, and placed it carefully on the lamp table as he turned to make the bed in sharp military corners, and thought of what he would need to take with him.

Chapter Two

Three days later, in Birmingham, Alabama, Lincoln Reeves's own life was turned upside down by the arrival of a letter. This one was delivered by a black man, though, with whom, if Lincoln had any enmity, he was unaware of it.

"Nice day, George," Lincoln said, meeting the man at his own rickety gate. Like everything else on the sharecropper's farm, it needed fixing. Like everything else, it would have to wait in line.

"They all the same to me, Mistah Reeves," George said, shaking his head. Lincoln tried to recall if he had ever seen the man smile, and came up empty. "One day goes intuh the next, and then th' nex' day come aftuh that."

"Whatever you say, George." Lincoln took his mail from the dour mailman and smiled. He looked at the slate-blue sky over the dusty field, the clouds, felt the almost spring-like warmth. As the mailman turned away, already shaking his head, Lincoln said, "Couple of months it'll be spring, and then I can get to planting. And won't *that* be fine, George?"

"Whatever you says, Mistuh Reeves," George said, continuing to shake his head as he went through the gate, closing it behind him. He chuckled slightly. "Whatever you says. You say hi to that wife and baby of yours, now, Mr. Reeves."

Lincoln watched the man retreat down the dusty road, then looked at the sky again. It *would* be fine. It certainly would. His first crop, on his own — well, *almost* his own — farm, and this was a fine day, and this was, after all, a fine life. Inside he heard Matty singing to the baby, and Lincoln had, at this moment, to admit to himself that he had done all right for himself. He had come about as far as he had wished, if not as far as he had hoped. And Thomas Mullin had told him — ordered him — to stay in the Army. What did the old man know? . . .

A moment later, glancing at the mail in his hand, Lincoln had a moment of wonder. Had he conjured Thomas Mullin up? For there, at the top of the thin stack of letters, was a crisply cornered letter from the Lieutenant, the first Lincoln had received in nearly a year. And here Lincoln had begun to worry about the old man, that things were slipping for him.

Lincoln thumbed the flap of the letter open, wincing at the ragged tear he was putting in it, almost waiting for Mullin to snap a comment at him:

"What's the matter, Trooper? Are you so *lazy* that you can't open an envelope properly? What if that envelope were evidence? What if you were *destroying* evidence?"

Reeves pulled the thin sheet out, laughing inwardly at his picture of the man he had conjured up. Even now, even at this distance in time and miles, Lieutenant Thomas Mullin still made Lincoln's back stiffen up in salute, his mind more alert. It was silly. . . .

Lincoln read the short note, and instantly felt himself go rigid and alert. Not so silly . . .

"Matty!" he called, already wincing at the fight he would have with his wife. He could only hope she would understand.

Resolutely, steeling himself for the confrontation to come, he mounted the creaking steps of the farmhouse, vowing to fix them as soon as he returned, opened the squeaking screen door to enter.

A day later, filled with guilt and remorse, he was packed and ready to go. Another fine day was dawning; it would be even warmer than yesterday, the temperature climbing perhaps into the sixties. Wonderful weather for January. There were a lot of chores that wouldn't get done today. . . .

"Matty," he said, unable to say anything else, holding his hands out in supplication. His carpetbag lay at his feet on the porch. In Matty's arms, the baby cooed and twisted, following the flight of an early morning crow cawing through the air over the near field.

"You say you'll be back before planting," Matty said solemnly.

"Matty, I promise. You can get Jedediah and Marcus to help until then. Jedediah knows how to fix things, the pump and such, and if by any chance I was late he could start the early plowing." Seeing her eyebrows go up he continued in a rush. "Though I know that won't be necessary. But . . . if it is, he'll do it. He owes me big, I got him started last year. And Marcus is good with the baby, and can run chores to town. Oh please, Matty, don't be mad at me."

"I'm not mad at you, Lincoln," she said evenly. "I'm mad at Thomas Mullin and the Army."

"Don't be, Matty."

"When the Army gets hold of you, it's the only thing can make you act like this. Everything else, you're your own man. I just can't understand why you have to drop your life and run. Especially to help some white man."

He reached out to take one of her hands, but instead, she shifted the baby from the crook of her other arm and handed it to him.

"Say good-bye to your papa, Washington," Matty said coldly. "Say good-bye to your papa who's leaving you to help some crazy old fool find a drunk *white* man's *Indian* daughter."

The baby cooed, looking up into Lincoln's face and smiling. Lincoln looked at Matty imploringly.

"Matty, I've told you. These are the only two men from the Army I would do this for. Sergeant Adams saved my *life*. And Lieutenant Mullin is — "

"Like a father to you," Matty finished. "I've only heard it a thousand times, Lincoln." Suddenly, as she saw him reach down for his bag, her tone softened.

He straightened up, handed the baby to her.

"I have to go, Matty," he said, turning away.

"Lincoln — " She put her hand on his arm, gripped him tight, turned him around.

He looked down at her. "Matty, I said I'm sor— "

"I know," she whispered, reaching up to kiss him. Suddenly she was crying. "I know, and I understand. But you have to be careful."

"Of course I'll be careful," he said. He brought his lips down to the baby's head and kissed his crown. "And you be careful, too."

When he looked back at Matty she was still crying. "Oh, Lincoln." she said, hugging him tight.

"I know, Matty, I know."

Gently, he pulled away from her, walked down the steps, and didn't look back until he was far away, across his sharecropped field, at the edge of the land that might one day be his or his son's.

When he looked back he waved, and Matty waved back, and made little Washington wave, too.

Chapter Three

Steel your mind, Thomas.

He hadn't remembered how truly tedious a long train trip could be. What at first began as an exciting excursion, a setting out for new places on a machine that traveled the rails faster than any man could run or ride, became, after the first few days, a boring series of embarkings and debarkings, facing an endless dull panorama of shorn trees and winter whiteness. What had at first been charming soon turned maddening, and Thomas was thankful for the thin stack of unread *Strand* magazines he had brought in his bag. He had particularly enjoyed Conan Doyle's most recent adventure, published in the December 1902 edition, recounting the "Adventare of the Speckled Band." Conan Doyle was back at his best, after a disastrous interlude where he had tried to kill Sherlock Holmes off, then, after an outcry which Thomas had only been too willing to add to, posting three letters in as many days to the *Strand* after they had dared to offer to the reading public the outrage titled "An Affair at Reichenbach Falls."

But the present adventure was more up to snuff, with Holmes employing all of his deductive powers to great end, and Thomas knew this Holmes story was a fine one because he had been unable to guess its ending. That had only happened once in the last year, a sure sign that Conan Doyle had been losing his powers.

Perhaps we're both coming back, Conan Doyle, he thought.

He shifted his weight on his bag, and looked out the window. The baggage car was empty now, another Negro having gotten off in Fort Worth. Only twice in the past two weeks had he sat in the last passenger car, but that was back in the East, where segregation was more subtle, and now that he was back in the South, the more overt forms of racism were evident. But baggage cars could be made comfortable, and the Negro porter on this train had taken good care of him, and made sure that he was fed properly and allowed to use the men's facilities after the white passengers had gone to bed for the evening. . . .

The window was small, and smudged, but it showed the same relentless vista of bleak winter, the same denuded trees, only mercifully shy of snow.

Thomas tucked his *Strand* magazine away and drew out the papers in his jacket pocket.

The first was the letter from Bill Adams, which he had been over numerous times. Always he came to the same conclusions. The second was a telegram from Lincoln Reeves, waiting for him in Kansas City, as he had instructed, with one word, *Yes.*

These two he put away, finding no more interest in them. The third, however, still held his attention. It was another telegram, this one from Tucson, from the landlord of the hotel where Bill Adams had been staying. Though it was few in words, it told Thomas much:

ADAMS BELIEVED DEAD STOP. INJUN BEING HELD STOP. MARSHAL SAYS NO ARMY INTERFERENCE NEEDED STOP. CATES.

Apparently Mr. Cates had misunderstood Thomas's own telegram, regarding his present status with the U.S. Army. That was fine, and irrelevant. Besides the fact that his friend might be dead, Thomas found he could read volumes from the short message.

First, it was obvious that Bill had gone after his daughter and was missing somewhere on the Papagos Reservation. This did not change Thomas's mission, but only made it more urgent. Bill Adams, despite his alcoholism, knew how to travel and how to survive. Thomas would reserve judgment on his death until he

27

had seen a body. Secondly, there was an Indian being held for Adams's supposed murder. This alone Thomas found curious, since Cates had stated that Bill was *believed* to be dead. And the Marshal who was handling this case had apparently decided that he didn't like Thomas already, based merely on the fact, however misinterpreted, that Thomas was an Army man. This implied friction with the local Army people. Nowhere had Thomas mentioned that he was Negro, and this fact was apparently not known. So the marshal, and Mr. Cates, would have a surprise for them when Thomas arrived.

But the most telling piece of paper Thomas had was one that didn't exist, the reply to his *second* telegram, which Thomas had sent from St. Louis, and which had never been answered. So Thomas had already been cut out of the loop, and would be on his own when he arrived.

Thomas put Cates's telegram away, and again looked out the smudged window.

The shorn trees of winter had been replaced, not by snow, but by the beginnings of Texas desert. This was a place he knew. A mere two hundred miles west lay Abilene, and another hundred miles to the south and west of that lay Fort Davis, which had been his home in the Army for so long.

He found himself sitting straighter, clearing the smudged window so he could look out. Already, west of Fort Worth, the trees were changing to desert oak, cottonwood, and mesquite brush. Winter had been left behind. Remembrance, and longing, flooded through him, and it occurred to him just how much he had missed this landscape. This land was like his soul, sparse and clean, and all the clutter of the East had only contributed to the crowding of his mind and the softening of his spirit. It was as if a spigot had been opened, letting out all the tarnish that had built up in him over the past five years, leaving only cold steel behind. He felt, if not young, then at least *himself* again.

He was home.

With a satisfied sigh, he turned away from the window and pulled out another copy of the *Strand* magazine from his bag. It was a story he had read many times before, the first installment of "The Hound of the Baskervilles," but he didn't care.

In the next hours, as light turned brighter with noon and then dimmer with evening, obliging him to hold the pages of the magazine to the window as he read, he was lost in a world that he loved and knew, and the words *steel yourself* did not enter his mind, because there was no need.

29

Chapter Four

In the high mountain, the one known as Oto-A-Pe, the sacred mountain, the eagle waited.

The eagle was patient. Its eyes were sharp, and its mind clear. The eagle saw all from its perch, and all that it saw, it ruled.

The eagle was a god.

And the people worshipped it. And feared it, for the eagle was a vengeful god, one to take measures against those who invited its wrath.

And the people below, the Tohono O'otam, whom the white man called the Papagos, had angered the eagle.

The Tohono O'otam were a peaceful people, but this did not concern the eagle. It did not care that they were at peace with themselves. The white man preyed on them, as did the Spanish before them. The eagle cared little for the gifts they left for it, the coiled baskets of devil's claw and yucca sewn over bear grass, the horsehair miniatures they left as tokens at the foot of its perch. The food they left, from their meagre cultivation of the flood plains below, it ate but did not taste. For the eagle had little but derision for the Tohono O'otam, whom it considered weak, and it had only anger for them in its heart.

They had tried to talk with the eagle, to assuage it, but this was to no avail. It was when the eagle had clawed their headman, the Keeper of the Smoke, who had come to speak with it, and whose body it had hurled to the rocks below for the council of old men to see, that the Tohono O'otam knew that its wrath was great, and that its anger for them was vast. It was then that it had swooped down on them, and bloodied one of their squaws in the night as she slept, and gave them the sign that it would only be assuaged if this sacrifice was brought to it at each sign of the moon. In their dreams, the eagle knew that they saw what it wanted to curb its wrath. And though there was much sad singing in the reservation below, and many tears, this is what they gave the eagle.

Tonight, on the night when the moon disappeared from the sky, they would give it to him again.

The eagle saw them, with its sharp eyes, by the light of many sharp stars, climbing the rocks below to leave what it demanded at the foot of its perch. Even now they moaned and sang. The new Keeper of the Smoke led them, declaiming the visions he had, and behind him

31

the old women circled the young squaw they would leave for the eagle. She was filled with dreams and smoke, the eagle saw. It wondered if they had given her white man's whiskey, for she stumbled in their midst, and spoke loudly, and even laughed. She did not act as she would if they had given her the doorway of dreams. This only made the old women moan louder, and the Keeper of the Smoke speak louder with his prayers, mixing the native with the prayers of the Catholic faith they had intermingled with their own beliefs, so that the eagle would not hear the squaw's laughter and become even more angry.

Anger stirred within the eagle and with it the momentary wish to swoop down and claw them all, but it held back, and only watched with its sharp eyes.

When they had come close enough for the eagle, it merely moved its feathered wings in the darkness, and they immediately halted below it.

The Keeper of the Smoke looked up, and there was fear in his eyes as he searched the darkness, trying to see the eagle.

The eagle, filled with loathing for the old man's weakness, waited quietly.

"Eagle god, ruler of Oto-A-Pe, ruler of the high mountain, and the vistas, and skies surrounding it, we have come!"

Though the old man tried to sound strong, the eagle could hear the trembling weakness in his voice.

"Great bird," the old man went on, "whose wrath is great and mighty, we have brought to you the gift you desire. We ask that now, this time, your anger with the Tohono O'otam be melted as the quick snow in the desert morning, and that peace return between you and the Tohono O'otam! We have only peace for you in our hearts, and wish for your vengeance to fly as you fly, strong and mighty, above the clouds!"

The eagle waited for a moment, hearing the old man's labored breathing at the height of the mountain and his fear, hearing the young squaw tittering, and the old women trying to quiet her.

"Great eagle," the Keeper of the Smoke said, "do you hear me?"

Now, the eagle merely fluttered its wings.

"The eagle hears," the old man said to the squaws, turning away.

The eagle relished the sadness in his voice. Again the eagle fluttered its feathered wings, and the Keeper of the Smoke said to the old women, "We must go."

The old women turned away, but then as the young squaw fell to her knees, laughing, one of the old women fell beside her, crying

33

and holding on to her. The squaw laughed, but the old woman held her tight, weeping, and crying to heaven.

The Keeper of the Smoke tried to make her let go of the squaw, but could not. "You must come with us, the eagle is angry," he said, but the old woman continued to moan, rocking the laughing squaw in her arms.

The eagle, relishing the moment, fluttered its wings in a wide arc.

"You must leave!" the Keeper of the Smoke cried.

But the old woman would not leave the squaw.

The eagle made a movement with its claw on the ground, and suddenly the old man below stood up and turned away. The other old women were already making their way hurriedly down the path to the rocks below.

The old woman continued to rock the squaw in her arms and weep.

Angered now, the eagle spread its wings and moved forward.

"For the last time, you must go!" the Keeper of the Smoke called out, stopping as he made his way down into darkness. The eagle thought with satisfaction of the bad night the Keeper of the Smoke and the old women would pass in the thin air below him, because they could not possibly make their way down the mountain in darkness.

"Come!" the Keeper of the Smoke ordered, but the old woman ignored him.

The squaw laughed, trying to push the old woman away.

Giving up, listening to the moaning warnings of the rest of the old squaws, the Keeper of the Smoke retreated.

The eagle waited, seeing with its sharp eyes the night, the sweeping plains far below, the hurrying figures of the Keeper of the Smoke and the old women, the dark moon, the thin, high clouds, the stars.

The young squaw laughed.

The eagle raised its wings high, fluttering its feathers and letting the cold air fill them, readied its claw, and swooped down.

As the eagle reached them, the old woman screamed. But the young squaw looked up at him, laughing, whiskey in her eyes, reaching out to stroke the eagle's feathers, and said, "Look, it flies like the wind!"

Hovering above them, the eagle looked down upon her with its sharp eyes for a moment.

Then the eagle's claw came down from the night upon them both. And the night of the dark moon was filled with cries of vengeance taken.

Chapter Five

Tucson was similar to Fort Davis, but different in subtle ways. They both shared desert characteristics, both shared the dry, clean air that Thomas had so forgotten about in humid Boston, but they were different pages from the same book. For one thing, Thomas had never seen saguaro cactus before. They were a species unknown to West Texas, and, indeed, he was told, by a crusty Negro miner named Coleman he had shared last leg of his interminable train trip into Tucson on the Southern Pacific Railroad with, unknown to the rest of the world. Saguaro climbed up hillsides in ranks, stood like sentries at the sides of roads, and indeed seemed to grow wherever they wished in the arid climate of Tucson.

The mountains, too, were different here. The Fort Davis area had been dominated by two ranges, the Eagle and Davis mountains, small chains that lay like dropped strings upon a table. Tucson itself lay at the curling bowl of a low mountain, and the area immediately surrounding was dotted by small peaks; it wasn't until one rode thirty to forty miles of flat territory through Indian reservation land that the real mountains began.

And the city of Tucson was, well, a city. Fort Davis had been little more than a few ranches and stores clustered for protection close around the fort itself; here was a growing, sprawling, flat expanse of construction that seemed as though it might never stop. The same Negro miner had pointed out the massive building, under construction, of St. Augustine Cathedral, and the cluster of buildings, like a child's unfinished block construction, of the University of Arizona. "Got to remember," the miner had said, "that ever since these here United States bought this piece of sand and rock in 1853, something called the Gadsden Purchase — they calls it the 'Godsend Purchase' around here — that they's been doing nothing but building. Prob'ly build right to the horizon 'fore they's finished. *If* they's ever finished." The miner held out, a final time as they stood on the platform of the station, his whiskey flask. "Sure you don' want a little? Gonna need it, being that color and not working for the white man 'round here. As for me, I sometimes wish I was back in Memphis, bad as that was."

Thomas had waved him off yet again, and asked for directions to the hotel run by Cates, who had sent him one telegram and neglected to send the second.

The man had told him where it was, then said, "You wants to be careful 'round them folks, friend." He clasped his hands tight around the whiskey flask. "They's tight 'round here, those white folks. And Mr. Cates is def'nitely one of 'em. Only white man I'd say you might trust is Marshal Murphy. Maybe."

The man had unclasped his hands, held the whiskey bottle out. "Sure?"

"I'm sure," Thomas had said, and walked toward the hotel, already feeling as if he had stepped into a nest of unknown snakes.

Cates's Hotel proved to be a much more elaborate affair than Thomas expected, with a gilded front and new tiled roof above its third floor. Biting back his pride, Thomas went around to the side entrance as he was expected to, and asked for Mr. Cates at the kitchen entrance. The cook, a short man who responded to Thomas's Spanish, told him to wait. He was gone for a long time. When he finally did return, he went back to his vegetable block and ignored Thomas completely.

"Excuse me," Thomas said.

"*No mas,*" the cook said, not looking at him.

In Spanish, Thomas asked if the cook had

told Mr. Cates he was here.

The cook ignored him, then seemed to sense his growing anger. Holding his knife a little tighter while he chopped, he finally said, "I tol' him, he said to make you go away."

"You tell Mr. Cates — " Thomas began, but then a large white man, in whiskers, with the jolly demeanor of a barkeep, was filling the doorway, and looking at Thomas.

"You can tell me yourself," he said gruffly. Then he turned away, into a side pantry, and waited for Thomas to follow.

The pantry proved to be larger than it looked from the street. Between the shelves of canned and jarred goods was a small desk covered with invoices, with a chair behind it. Thomas noted an Abercrombie and Fitch catalog on the desk, which Cates pushed aside. Cates sat down in the chair. There was nowhere else in the room to sit.

"As soon as I told Miguel to make you disappear, I knew it was a mistake," he said. Before Thomas could attempt to thank him, he continued, "From what Bill Adams told me, you were a pushy little bulldog, and wouldn't take no for an answer."

Again Thomas tried to open his mouth, but Cates rolled on.

"I should apologize for not answering that second telegram of yours. But I saw no need to. Figured you were smart enough to figure the story out and didn't need no a second time." Cates sighed. "I was wrong."

This time. Thomas didn't even try to speak.

"You've got to realize something, Mullin. The Bill Adams I knew, and the one you knew, were two different people. Adams was a major drinker by the end, and half the time he didn't know what he was telling and who he was telling it to.

"I was in the Army, too, Fort Collins up in Wyoming. Which is why I'm being so civil. I understand you made it to lieutenant. That's quite an achievement, for your race. I can't say I ever knew even a Mexican made it that far, never mind one of you people. I also hear you knew Grierson, back in Washington, which couldn't have hurt."

For the first time, Cates bothered to look straight at Thomas, and Thomas saw just how hard his face was behind the jovial whiskers.

"This ain't the army, and you ain't a lieutenant anymore," he said. "And I thought even a smart darkie like you're supposed to be would figure out you're not wanted in Tucson."

Holding his temper, Thomas said evenly, "If you'll just tell me where Bill Adams was heading, I'll be on my way."

Cates rose slowly to his full height and

walked around the desk. He brought his face close to Thomas's and said angrily, "Maybe I didn't make myself clear — "

"Trouble, Dexter?" came a mild voice from the doorway.

They both turned to face a tall, thin man leaning on the doorjamb leading into the pantry with his arms crossed. He was almost boyish looking, with red hair and a thin, reddish beard. His eyes were as mild as his voice. He seemed to be waiting for Cates to say something, a questioning look on his face.

"Murphy," Cates said, not happily.

When Murphy stood straight, uncrossing his arms, Thomas saw the Marshal's badge pinned to his shirt.

"I was passing by, heard a ruckus," Murphy said. He put his thumbs in his belt, and again the questioning look crossed his face.

"Actually," Cates said, "I caught this darkie trying to steal from my pantry. Ain't that right, Miguel?" Cates called out to the cook, who stared down at his chopping block, making furious chops with his knife, trying to ignore what was going on in the pantry.

"Ain't that *right*, Miguel?" Cates repeated, raising his voice."

"*Si*, whatever you say, Mr. Cates," Miguel said, coloring. The chopping became even more furious. "Whatever you say."

41

Cates turned his even look on Murphy.

Murphy took his thumbs from his belt, stretched his arms over his head, and then let them fall to his side. One had brushed a gunbelt, and the .45 holstered in it. "Well, then" — Murphy smiled amiably — "I guess this here fellah ought to come with me." Murphy gestured to the Abercrombie and Fitch catalog. "By the way, Dexter, they got a package for you down by the railroad yard from that sporting goods outfit."

Cates blinked his eyes, said, "Thank you, Marshal."

Murphy looked at Thomas, smiled, turned, and walked out.

Thomas gave Cates a hard look and followed, as Cates laughed behind him.

"Don't worry, Darkie, we got a *good* work program here! Thirty days in the copper mines do you good!" He laughed again.

Outside, Thomas saw Murphy gesture to him lazily at the mouth of the alley. When Thomas reached the street, the lawman was halfway up the block, crossing to an office with a U.S. Marshal sign over it.

Without looking, Murphy entered, leaving the door open behind him.

Thomas stalked across the street, into the office, only to flnd it seemingly empty. Then, from a small room off to one side, he heard the sound of rushing water. In a moment, Murphy appeared, stopping to give him his mildly questioning look.

"Sit down, Mr. Mullin," he said, gesturing to the desk and the visitor's chair in front of it. Murphy nodded at the little room behind him. "First lawman west of the Brazos River to have a toilet in my office. 'Least that's what a newspaper man through here last September told me he was going to write. Back East, they don't seem to give a spit whether it's true or false, 'long as it's colorful. This time, at least, it's true."

He ambled his long frame over behind his desk, sat down, and lifted one long leg up onto the desk. He put his hands behind his head, leaned back in his swivel chair, and peered at Thomas lazily.

"Now, what can I do for you?"

"You heard what Cates — " Thomas began angrily, but a wave of Murphy's hand silenced him.

"Hell with Mr. Cates," Murphy said. "I had a quick talk with Miguel coming into the kitchen. He told me the truth. This way, he can say whatever Cates wants and not lose his job." His eyes seemed to focus a little more sharply. "I hear you're here to look for Bill Adams."

"That's right."

"You're his army buddy, right?"

"That's correct, marshal."

"Cates tell you he was dead?"

"He implied it, in a telegram."

"Well, Bill Adams sure ain't dead. Indian name of Tahini, works for one of the mining companies, saw him in the Baboquivari Mountains last week. They had a drink, talked for a while. Adams was coming down off one peak, heading up to another."

"Cates told me an Indian was being held for Bill's murder."

Murphy laughed. "That's a hoot! I had Tahini in the drunk tank here, and that ain't the first time that's happened. No, Mr. Mullin, your friend is just fine. At least as of last week."

"Marshal," Thomas said carefully, "can I ask you why no search party was sent to find Bill Adams's daughter?"

Murphy took his hands from behind his head and leaned forward until his arms were resting on his desk. The detached look disappeared from his face. When Murphy was serious, Thomas noted, he looked a lot less boyish.

"Mr. Mullin, no search party was needed."

"May I ask — "

"Because Abby Adams left on her own to return to the Papagos reservation, where she

44

was raised. Her father couldn't take the fact that she didn't want to live here in Tucson with him. Mostly, I imagine, he couldn't take the fact that she was more Indian than white. He tried to dress her up in fancy clothes, teach her to keep house, all of that, but it just didn't take on the girl. Even when she went to church she was more Indian than white, singing that sing-song way they have while everyone else is trying to muddle through their hymns." He leaned farther forward on the desk. "Sorry, Mr. Mullin, but I just don't see a mystery here myself."

Thomas said, "Cates also mentioned something about your not wanting 'Army interference.'"

"Don't know what he meant by that, except for the fact that we got a little Apache trouble down in those mountains where your friend is now, and the Army keeps refusing to help with it. Hell, I'd *love* to get me a bit of Army help, instead of forming a posse filled with shopkeepers every time an Apache steals a couple of ranch horses. The Apaches bother the Papagos sometimes, but that's none of our business. One thing you've got to know about the Papagos, or Tohono O'otam, as they call themselves, and that's that they're pretty peaceful Indians. The mining companies and ranchers have stolen a lot of their land, but

45

they're more afraid of the Apaches than of the white man, so there hasn't been much trouble with them. About the biggest problem up there now is peyote, which they've starting using to dream. Dreams tell them everything, how to live, what to do. I've heard rumors about some kind of eagle attacking some of their young women, maybe even killing a couple of them. I wouldn't be surprised if that's what your friend Adams is worried about. Unfortunately, like I said, it's none of my business, or the government's. You think Washington gives a damn about that reservation anymore? Hell, Roosevelt's busy worrying about Spain and Cuba, and all that rot. Don't know if you heard it, but we've got the President coming out here Saturday. But that's just politics, he's just making campaign stops on a swing through the West. Reckon that'll keep me plenty busy. But you can bet there won't be any talk of Indian trouble when Roosevelt comes here. Far as Washington's concerned, Arizona is closed as far as Indian trouble goes."

Thomas got up. "Thank you, Marshal."

Murphy uncoiled his lanky frame and stood up. "No problem, Mr. Mullin. Anything I can do for you, you let me know. Way I see it, what you have is a buddy who's had himself one too many drinks and needs to be brought

46

home. I like Bill Adams, he never gave me much trouble until recently, when he started to tilt the bottle too much. He told me all about you, the couple times I had him in here to dry out. He thought you could have made one hell of a lawman if . . ."

For the first time, Thomas saw the Marshal become uneasy.

"If not for my skin color, Marshal."

To his surprise, the thin man reached out to take his hand.

"Take care of yourself, Mr. Mullin, and I do mean be careful. I'll try to see that Cates gives you no trouble, though I can't understand why he had a stake in the matter to begin with. You wouldn't believe it by the way Cates struts around, but he used to be a poor man until recently. This town's population has nearly doubled in three years, and Cates has managed to make his hotel one of the most desirable in Tucson." He laughed. "Though I can't say the proprietor is too likable."

At the door to the office, Thomas stopped and turned around.

"Marshal, is there any chance I could talk to Tahini?"

Murphy had settled himself back into his chair. "If you can find him. He left the city 'bout a week ago, soon as I let him out. Had a surveying job to finish. That fellow can drink, and he can survey land. I'll give him that." Murphy pondered. "You could probably find him out around the foot of Kitt Peak, in the Baboquivaris. That's where he told me he was heading. But I'd be real careful out there, because that's where we've been having Apache trouble."

"Thank you again, Marshal."

"Like I said, anytime. And Mr. Mullin."

"Yes, Marshal?"

"Don't get the idea that we're all like Cates around here. I may be wrong, and I probably am, but I like to think that in Tucson we look at a man's deeds first, and his color second." Murphy frowned. "Hell, that sounded like hogwash even coming out of my mouth." He put his thumbs down to his gunbelt. "Take care with yourself, Mr. Mullin."

"I will, Marshal. I will."

Chapter Six

At the foot of Kitt Peak, Oto-A-Pe, the Sacred Mountain, Tahini made the sign of the cross. He also said the prayers of The People, the chant to the Great Spirit of dreams, and the invocation of the Eagle, which made him shudder, the stories he'd been hearing. If he had known any other religious invocations, he would have added them, too, because the Sacred Mountain was very sacred indeed, the most sacred of all mountains to the Tohono O'otam. The very fact that he was at the base of the sacred place without permission from the Council or the Keeper of the Smoke made him nervous — but money, and much whiskey from the copper mining people, helped to ease his worry, and do his job. He had heard Frawley tell the big boss, Mates, that he was the best surveyor they had, and though Tahini had not let on that he had heard them, he had tucked it away in his mind for the future. When the next surveying job came along, he was sure he could extract even more pay — and more whiskey — from the bosses. Then everyone would be happy, right?

For wasn't happiness the way of the whiskey? Time to test it, he thought. He uncapped his flask and tipped it back, letting the amber liquid slide down his throat. Though it was just noon, he had already done this three or four times, and would continue to do it until the flask, and the new bottle he had filled it with, were gone. Then tomorrow he would open another bottle, and so on, until all the bottles were gone and the job was finished. Then he would ride back to the mining camp, twenty miles away, and talk to Jellek and the other boss about the next job, and the next pay, and supply of whiskey.

Happiness . . .

He felt the warm amber settle in his stomach and open like a sunrise through his blood. He imagined this was what heaven was like. Though there would be hell to follow, when the hangover hit him hours from now . . .

Happiness . . .

For now, though, there was only happiness. He took another quick sip of the liquid, capped the flask, and put it away in his trousers. There was nothing like the white men's trousers, with all of its pockets, for holding things.

Happiness . . .

Reluctantly, he left the flask in its pocket and reached into another one, in the back, drawing out Jellek's map. It was near here, Tahini was sure, that they wanted him to use his instruments. He studied the area closely, then walked, with a slightly unsteady step, to the surveying instruments already set up in alignment. He sighted through the scope, checked the map again.

Yes, this was it.

For the next twenty minutes, the whiskey bottle was forgotten while Tahini worked. But that did not mean part of his mind wasn't on it while he measured, and staked the ground, and measured again. By the end of the twenty minutes he was thirsty indeed, and finally, as he peered blurrily through the sextant, forgetting exactly what stretch of staked-out dirt he was supposed to be looking at, he jammed the map into his back pocket, reaching around to the front pocket to retrieve the whiskey flask. Still looking through the instrument, he uncapped the flask and brought it up —

Something was blocking the front of the sextant.

Suddenly, the flat expanse of dirt, the painted stake, went away. A shadow passed before the instrument, and now Tahini saw only blackness. Immediately, he thought of the Sacred Mountain. He stumbled back away from the machine. *White man's fool-*

ishness, he thought. Now he would pay for his sins. . . .

But there was no darkness surrounding Kitt Peak, no thunderous rage of gods ready to fall on him.

Someone had thrown a coat over the end of the sextant's telescope.

"Hey, Tahini!" a voice called, laughing.

"Bill!" he answered, beginning to breathe again.

Bill Adams smiled at him from ear to ear, standing in front of the instrument. He plucked his coat off the sextant, threw it down, and sat on it. Already, he was uncapping his own bottle.

"Hope you're not mad at me, Tahini," Adams said amiably.

"Hell, no, Bill, you just gave me a turn is all."

Adams laughed. "Here, have a drink."

"Don't mind if I do."

Tahini sat next to the white man on his coat and took the bottle. Adams was looking at him.

"Say, I did send you for a loop, didn't I?"

"Yes, you did." Tahini smiled, taking the bottle from Adams's outstretched hand.

"Never drink alone, and never drink your own, eh, Tahini?" Adams laughed.

"Say, Bill," Tahini said, frowning after he had taken a long drink.

Adams waited for him to continue.

Tahini suddenly turned to the white man, staring. "Say, Bill, you all right?"

"Why wouldn't I be all right, Tahini?"

"What you doing out here, Bill? You shouldn't be near Kitt Peak. I hear there's all kinds of weird things happening out here lately."

A frown crossed Adams's face; he looked as though he was trying to remember something. "Don't know. . . ."

"Bill, where you just come from?"

"Why . . ." Again a frown crossed Adams's face. He suddenly looked up at the Indian and smiled. "Can't quite remember that, Tahini. Talked to the Great Spirit, I think." He pointed up.

"Oh, boy."

"Say, Tahini," Adams said, looking up at the Indian questioningly. "You think I'm lying? I'm telling you, I just found out many interesting things." He frowned. "If only I could remember what they were."

Drunk as he was, Tahini knew that something was very much wrong. Rising unsteadily, he approached Bill Adams's mount, which stood patiently in the shade of a rock outcrop. Rifling through the saddlebags, he found the remains of Adams's provisions — a few days' worth of food, a blanket, a tobacco pouch.

"Bill," he called back, "where's your ammo, your rifle?"

There was no answer.

"Say, Bill — "

When he looked back, the white man was slumped over on his side of the coat, unmoving.

"Oh, Jesus spirit," Tahini said.

When he reached Adams, there was a faint pulse in the neck. Turing the white man over, he cradled Adams's head in his lap.

"Bill . . ."

Adams's eyes fluttered open. He stared straight through Tahini, and there was a sudden look of horror on his face. He clutched the Indian's collar, tried to raise himself.

"Settle down there, Bill," Tahini said gently.

"You tell me *what!*" Adams said, his eyes wide. "This isn't true! None of it is true!"

"Say, Bill — "

Adams ignored him. "I'll get the Army! I'll get Sherlock Holmes himself after you!"

Adams let go of Tahini and fell back. He seemed to be listening. Then, suddenly, he screamed, and his eyes opened impossibly wide, and he began to thrash in Tahini's grip.

"No! No!" Adams cried, trying to cover his face.

"Bill — "

"Get Thomas Mullin — " Adams went suddenly limp, collapsing in Tahini's arms.

Tahini once again checked for a pulse.

There was none.

"Jesus spirit . . ."

He lay Adams's body back on the ground. The man's neck was rigid, his head thrown back, his mouth locked open in a scream he would never make. His eyes were nearly bulging out of his head.

Hands shaking, Tahini grabbed for Adams's bottle, which had rolled away, half-spilled on the ground. He brought it to his lips, closed his eyes, and drank until warm numbness spread through him.

Jesus, he thought, *they'll blame you for sure now. They already had you once and let you go; this time they'll stick you in that cell and close the door forever. Or hang you by your neck.*

Lowering the bottle, seeing that it was empty, he stood, and looked down at Bill Adams's body.

Sorry, old friend, but I've got to do this. Got to do it for me.

Retrieving the shovel from his own pack, he found a place off under the rocks, and began to dig.

Two hours later, as the sun was starting to fall toward the west, Tahini was done. The grave was Indian style, shallow, covered with rocks. Then he shielded the front of the rock overhang with larger rocks, blending it into the scenery. He would tell Jellek this spot was no good for the road they wanted, steer him to one of the alternates. Tomorrow he would survey an appropriate spot and head back to camp. With any luck, they would never find Bill Adams.

Inappropriately, Tahini found himself crying. Adams's own bottle had long since been emptied, and he had the remains of his own, sitting cross-legged on the ground, facing the sun. Closing his eyes, he said all the prayers he knew, Christian and otherwise, praying for forgiveness and guidance. He ended by asking the Great Spirit to guide his steps.

Rising unsteadily, as the sun lipped the far horizon, he approached Bill Adams's mount, untied it from its spot under a rock overhang, and slapped it across the flanks to make it run.

"Gallop far, my friend," he said, bringing the bottle back up to his lips again.

Above him, on the rock overhang, he heard a sound. A few pebbles clattered down, falling nearby.

Tahini looked up.

"Great Spirit . . ." he mumbled. Then, his eyes widening, "No . . ."

56

Something tall and wide spread its wings above him.

"Oh, no," Tahini said.

As the thing dropped down upon him in a flutter of feathers, he held the empty bottle out futilely in defense and supplication.

Chapter Seven

Lincoln Reeves felt more than a sense of annoyance.

I should have known, he thought. *I should have known the old man would take off without me.*

Adjusting himself on the saddle, Lincoln thought about just how long it had been since he had ridden a horse like this. Five years. In the past year, since he had taken over the sharecropper's farm, the only horses he had dealt with had been tied to a wagon or a plow. It made him feel inadequate, settled, and strangely old.

Old, at twenty-eight.

He laughed.

Sore butt tonight.

He had been lucky to find Marshal Murphy waiting for him at the station. If Murphy hadn't been there, he might have gone to Gates at the hotel, and from what Murphy had diplomatically told him that would have been a bad move. But Murphy had seemed like a decent sort, and the very fact that Lieutenant Mullin had trusted the lawman to meet him and tell him where Thomas was headed was enough for Reeves. He tried to be madder at Thomas Mullin but found himself incapable of more than annoyance.

The old man could have waited for me.

Thinking on that, he knew how foolish it was. Thomas would have wanted to get moving right away, not hang around in Tucson, pretty as it was. Reeves promised himself he would see the sights before he left, after this business was over.

Momentarily, guilt assaulted him, thinking of his wife and child. He hadn't even sent the telegram he'd promised when he got in, just picked up the saddled and provisioned mount Thomas provided for him, and headed out.

I'll have to send that telegram as soon as I can.

Once again, he was torn between home and here. It was a hard thing to admit to himself that he missed this life. In a way, he even missed the Army. If Lieutenant Mullin had stayed in the Army, he knew he might very well have stayed with him, despite Matty's wishes. But that was something, thank heaven, that he didn't have to agonize over, since the Army eased Thomas out as soon as Grierson retired. Though they'd done it gently enough, and made it look grand, it had been obvious to everyone that Captain Seavers, now back in Washington after his disastrous tenure at Fort Davis, had used all his power — or at least all the power that his own marriage to a general's daughter had given him — to eject Thomas as quickly and ignominiously as possible. It had all left a bad taste in everyone's mouth, since, if there had been any justice in the world, Thomas would have had a command instead of an honorable discharge. . . .

Ride, Lincoln, don't think.

But thinking was part of what he missed. In the time he had been with Lieutenant Mullin, he had learned how to read, and how to think. Thomas's was the sharpest mind he had ever met, and the man was a marvel. He looked at the world under a microscope, and saw things no one else did.

Which reminded Reeves that Lieutenant Mullin had ridden out without him.

Couldn't wait an extra day for me.

Laughing, feeling already at home in the saddle despite his sore butt muscle, Reeves kicked the mount forward to find his old friend.

But by nightfall, he hadn't done that. He had found the markers on the map Thomas left with Murphy easily enough, but there was no sign of the old man there. He had expected a camp, but found only saguaro cactus and smooth desert plain. The Baboquivari mountains lay in the distance, rising shadows out of the coming night, and Lincoln felt suddenly alone. His annoyance with Thomas threatened to turn to anger, a feeling easier to deal with than the growing apprehension he felt, a black man in a strange area alone. . . .

Think, Lincoln. Think.

He could almost hear the old man speaking to him. Thomas might have been impulsive, but he wasn't foolhardy or unkind. Even if he had been here and gone, he would have left signs.

Think.

Lincoln dismounted at the spot indicated between two low hills, hugging the one on the right. There was a ring of cactus nearby, just as on the map, a virtual planter's field of saguaro marching up the shallow hillside. He was sure he was in the right place.

Think.

He tethered the horse to a nearby cactus and stood examining the landscape in the failing light. At worst, he would stay here the night and go on in the morning. But go on to where? Thomas *had* to have left a sign.

After a frustrating half hour of scouring the patch of land, by the end crawling on his hands and knees, Reeves was ready to give up and settle in for the night. Only a sliver of sun lay above the horizon, and soon that would be gone.

Lincoln kicked at the ground in frustration.

Suddenly, the line Thomas was always quoting, from Sherlock Holmes, rose into Lincoln's mind.

After you have eliminated the impossible, whatever remains, however improbable, must be the truth.

"Ah," Lincoln said, to no one in particular, feeling foolish even as he said it.

But what was impossible?

Plenty.

Already growing frustrated, as he did every time he tried to think like Thomas Mullin, Lincoln again kicked the ground.

After you have eliminated the impossible . . .

Well, it was impossible that Thomas would have left him out here on his own, wasn't it? Unless there was a damned good reason. What would that reason be?

He had found Adams.

But still, he would have left a clue as to his whereabouts. Unless he had found Adams at this exact spot, and was already heading back to Tucson to celebrate.

No . . .

Again Lincoln kicked the ground. His head hurt.

The sun was almost gone.

Lincoln raised his eyes to watch the departing light. There in his line of vision was a nest of cactus, three or four in an almost straight line. Lincoln stepped slightly to the left, and now the cactus was in a straight line.

And something was fluttering from the arm of one of them.

"Ha!"

Just as the sun dipped below the west, Lincoln tore the piece of paper, which had been speared on one of the cactus's pricks, and held it out to read. In the glow of twilight, he slowly made out the words, reading them aloud in the way Thomas had first taught him to read:

DUE WEST ELEVEN MILES, THEN DUE SOUTH THREE. MEET YOU AT THE BASE OF KITT PEAK 2/14. WILL WAIT. MULLIN.

"Ha!" Lincoln shouted, and this time was filled with pride for his accomplishment, small as it had been. He also felt sure that this area was secure, or Thomas would not have let him stay here on his own.

So something important had happened, and Thomas had gone off in search of it.

And tomorrow he would meet up with his old friend.

Washed in relief, Lincoln broke down his saddlebags and made a simple camp. In a little while, a small fire was crackling, and Lincoln was finishing the remains of canned beans, sitting on his bedroll. It was just like the old days.

In the night, old desert sounds returned to him, and he felt at home.

With only a little guilt, Lincoln remembered that he had forgotten to send that telegram, and that there would be hell to pay from Matty when he got back to his real home.

Chapter Eight

Under the stretching, infinite, pale blue bowl of the desert sky, Thomas Mullin felt liberated. His mind had not been clearer in years. He thought of Sherlock Holmes, entrenched in his stuffy chambers at 221B Baker Street, and wondered how Conan Doyle could ever fool his readers into thinking Holmes could solve anything. Wreathed in pipe smoke, hemmed in by claustrophobia, Thomas knew that he himself would merely go mad.

But to each his own.

Two days in the saddle, and he already felt ten years younger. Boston seemed like a bad dream now, a nightmare interlude in what had been a life of action. A man makes his own world, Thomas decided; starting from inside his head and working his way out to the physical world. For Holmes, his stuffy apartments were merely the props that made his own inner world comfortable; for Thomas himself, the wide expanse of the desert made his own mind sharp and content. It was something he had never realized; and he knew now that he would never return to the life he had been leading in Boston. For him, this infinite sky and dry dust of land was the key to his youth of mind and his mental health.

Murphy's warnings to take care had so far proved needless. The two men he had met, one white, one Indian, had proven friendly and unheedful of his color. The white man had, indeed, been a former army scout, and after introductions, he and Thomas had quickly fallen to swapping names and postings. It had turned out they had at least five friends in common, two retired, the other three still active in northwest duty. And they both shared similar concerns about Theodore Roosevelt.

The Indian had proved less chummy, but more useful as far as Thomas's present task was concerned. He not only knew the surveyor, Tahini, but knew where to find him. They worked for the same mining concern, and the Indian, named Kohono-si, had provided Thomas with exact directions. It would only take another half-day's ride to reach the spot where Tahini was presently working.

When Thomas had thanked Kohono-si for the information, the man had merely grunted and said, "If you go there, be guarded. I told Tahini this, too."

"What do you mean?" Thomas had asked, but Kohono-si had merely grunted again, mounted his horse, and ridden in the opposite direction.

As the ride would bring Thomas into nightfall, he was faced with a dilemma. Since he had originally thought Tahini would be in the area he had written Reeves about, he had the option of waiting for Lincoln or riding on ahead. Though filled with impatience, he had decided to be fair and wait for the young man. He didn't quite admit to himself that he wanted his young Watson's company, which was true.

But Kohono-si had changed his mind. A half hour after Thomas himself had reached the cactus-ridden spot of their meeting, the Indian had ridden up, stopped his horse, and stood staring down at Thomas.

"Something wrong?" Thomas had asked.

The Indian looked troubled, yet unwilling to speak.

"You wouldn't be here if you didn't have something to tell me."

"You are the man who fought Pretorio," Kohono-si said solemnly.

"That's right," Thomas said. It occurred to him that his mount was ten feet away, with his rifle in its sling.

"I salute you for that," Kohono-si said.

When nothing else was forthcoming, Thomas said, "Thank you."

Kohono-si still seemed to be battling himself. He looked off to the mountains in the near distance. "Pretorio was a bad chief, and his braves killed many of the Tohono O'otam."

"I know that. He killed many braves of many tribes."

Kohono-si grunted. Continuing to look off toward the mountains, he said, "But he is dead, and this is today. Because you are a friend of the Tohono O'otam, I want to warn you that the eagle is in the sacred mountain. The eagle is angry with the Tohono O'otam."

Now he finally looked at Thomas. "Be careful of the eagle. He resides in the sacred mountain, Oto-A-Pe, the one you call Kitt Peak. Do not anger the eagle."

Thomas scratched his chin and said, slowly, "Kohono-si, are the Tohono O'otam going on the warpath?"

Kohono-si looked away, toward the mountains. "This I cannot say. But I know the eagle is angry with Tahini. Tahini was to be on the Council of Elders, and he shunned this for the white man's job and liquor. The eagle is angry."

"Kohono-si, is the white man named Adams near where Tahini is working?"

"This is all I will say."

With that, the brave turned and rode away.

Thomas, analyzing the conversation, quickly left Lincoln Reeves a message and set out toward the spot where Tahini would be.

With a hard ride, Thomas still reached the area after nightfall. It was too late to do anything, so he made camp in a secure place, covered on three sides by rock outcroppings. He made a small fire and ate his dinner. Then he read by firelight for a while, a dog-eared copy of the *Strand* magazine containing an old Holmes story, "The Adventure of the Copper Beeches." He knew the story nearly by heart, and found his mind wandering away from it to stare at the drawings accompanying it.

He was thinking about Bill Adams. There was more to this story than Adams had let on. Though it was obvious that Adams cared for his daughter, in the years Thomas had known the man, he had only spoken of her three or four times. Once he had even referred to her as a 'half-breed.' That didn't preclude his love for her, but Adams's reaction to her going back to her natural home could not be the whole story.

And there was something eerie about this place. Thomas recalled the feeling he had had once, in the Davis mountains, when the cry of a deranged man had led him, briefly, to superstitious thoughts. Then, he had berated himself for those thoughts, because they were something Holmes would never feel. And though in the end the superstitions had turned out to be based all too much on reality, to this day the tinge of mysticism itself, he was convinced, had been something tangible. Holmes would not agree; to that rapier-like mind, everything could be reduced to the everyday; but Thomas was not so sure that things were so black and white. Was there an afterlife? He didn't know, and didn't much care. The question was, was reality a wider concept than Sherlock Holmes would be willing to accept? Were the boundaries of the real world wider, and softer at the edges, than the great fictional detective would admit? Though the Hound of the Baskervilles had turned out to be nothing more than a poor, starved animal, was there something to the feelings the beast had engendered in those he had frightened so terribly?

Thomas didn't know. But he was determined to keep an open mind.

And that feeling was with him again.

Analyze it, he thought. *Let it fill your mind, and pick it apart, and see what it is.*

He put down his magazine, and closed his eyes. His ears were sharp, his fingers so sensitive that the merest desert breeze tingled across them. He heard no cry of eagles, no cry of a deranged man, even, but still, there was something there, something tilted at the edge of the world. . . .

Bah. He opened his eyes, and decided that unless he could feel this thing, grasp it tightly with his own hands, it would remain to him only a vague concept. Holmes's way, the way that Thomas led most of his life, might very well be closer to the truth.

He turned, saw the outline of a prone human body not four feet from where he had left his horse.

Momentarily, a chill rose up his back, but he suppressed it.

He rose and approached the body. An Indian lay face down at the base of one of the rocks hemming in Thomas's camp. The arms were outstretched. In the flicker of firelight, Thomas could see vague lines running up the arms toward the hands.

He bent closer.

The lines were scratches; on closer examination, deep gashes.

Rummaging for a stick, Thomas bent closer and hooked the man's sleeve up. The gashes stopped near the elbow line.

The man's face was turned away from him. Thomas climbed over the body and bent close. Cursing at the bad light, he ran back to the

71

fire and fed it with kindling until it burned brighter. Then he returned to the body.

The face was marked with gashes, also.

Carefully, touching only clothing, Thomas turned the body over.

The front of the Indian's tunic was covered with deep cuts. So were the palms of the hands. He had tried to ward off his attacker until he had fallen. Most of the work had then been done on the chest, deep slicing cuts that had gutted and bled the body. They were not the sharp strokes of a knife blade, however, but wider, more ragged.

Thomas rose, fed the fire again, and examined the area around the body.

Nearby, knocked over, was a surveying instrument, its lenses shattered. There was no sign of a horse or saddlebags, but Thomas did find, near the base of the rocks, two liquor bottles, one empty, one nearly so, different brands.

Two bottles.

Thomas thought it unlikely that this one man, Tahini, he assumed, had consumed nearly two bottles of liquor. That alone would have killed him. Which meant there had been someone else with him.

Thomas recalled Murphy's information that Tahini and Bill Adams were friends.

Alive with the scent now, Thomas returned

to the fire and fed it every scrap of bush, weed, and stunted tree he could find, until it roared dangerously high. He kicked his copy of the *Strand* back just as flames were licking at it, and kicked his bedroll back away from the blaze, also.

He returned to the base of rocks. Climbing atop the lowest rock shelf, he examined the area around him. A series of rock shelves led up to a low ridge, which flattened out and gently sloped down to the desert floor. At the edge of the rock shelf, overlooking the spot where he had found Tahini, were scratches on the rock.

He examined the cracks around the rocks, found nothing.

Scrambling down to the desert floor, he looked into the shallow cuts formed by butting rocks, starting at one end and working his way down to the other. Where he could not see, he first poked in with a stick, to ward off snakes, then felt around with his hand.

Near the far side, after scaring a copperhead off, his hand reached between two close-butted rocks, and felt cloth.

He rose, and felt around the edge of the facing rock. It had been fitted into place.

Grunting with effort, he tried to pry it back, then discovered that it could be rolled aside.

Inside, swaddled in blankets, was a body.

He knew even before uncovering it that it was Bill Adams. Logic told him that it was. But the shock of seeing his old friend frozen in death, a grimace of horror on his face, still sent Thomas staggering back to gain a breath of air. Quickly, though, he reentered the shallow cave and dragged the body out.

There were no outward marks on Adams. So the two men had been killed in different ways.

Leaving Adams's body, Thomas went back to his search.

He found nothing else in the shallow cave, but found what he was looking for a few yards to the right of it. A tobacco pouch that he himself had given Bill on his fiftieth birthday. It had the initials W.A. burned into the leather.

Moving close to the fire, Thomas bent to the ground and opened the pouch up.

There was no tobacco inside. He turned the pouch over and nothing fell out, but, feeling down with his fingers, there was something adhering to the bottom.

He turned the pouch inside out, and a small, grayish, mushroom-shaped button fell to the desert floor.

Thomas picked it up, examined it, brought it close to his nose.

"So," he said, looking sadly down at the

body of his friend.

He let the fire burn down as he packed.

It was after sunrise when he was ready to head out, the two blanketed bodies lashed to his horse as he led it back toward where he had left the note for Lincoln Reeves. With any luck, young Reeves would already be on his way out, which would save Thomas from the long ride back. Though, even if he had to walk the entire way, he would have plenty to occupy his mind.

So engrossed was he in thought, then, that he didn't see Lincoln Reeves until the young man was nearly upon him.

"Lieutenant!" Lincoln called, stopping to hail Thomas from his saddle a quarter mile away. "Hey, Lieutenant!"

Thomas noted how Reeves kept shifting on his mount, and was able to pull himself up from his cognition long enough to laugh to himself. It was good to see his young Watson again.

He only wished it had been under happier circumstances.

Chapter Nine

"The problem," Murphy said, "is not that I don't believe you. I do. But as far as the law is concerned, the case is closed."

Thomas said, "If you don't mind my saying, Marshal, that's one hell of a way for law to work. There are two murders here, plain and simple, and you're telling me there's nothing you can do?"

They were in the Tucson City morgue, the first Thomas or Lincoln had ever been in. The room was in the basement of the hospital, little more than an underground storage room. Gas lamps flickered on the walls; one half of the room was filled with discarded hospital equipment, surplus gurneys, and instrument cases that looked as if they dated back to the War Between the States. The other half of the room displayed four rickety tables, a crude overhead electric light that flickered and then went out when Marshal Murphy attempted to turn it on, and a few white sheets piled in one corner. The ceiling was low and hollow; upstairs they could hear the comings and goings of nurses, and doctors going about their business.

"I didn't say there's nothing I can do. I just said that *officially* there's nothing I can do."

"I see," Thomas said. He turned to Lincoln, who stood back in the shadows, away from the twin tables holding the bodies. "Just like the Army, eh, Trooper Reeves?"

"Yes, sir," Lincoln said, a sick smile crawling over his features.

"What's the matter, Trooper? Don't you like it down here?"

"No, sir," Reeves said truthfully.

"Why not?"

"Reminds me of places my grandmother told me about. The Underground Railroad. She took me to one, once."

"Hmmm," Thomas said. He turned back to Murphy. "So what can you do, *unofficially?*"

Murphy smiled slightly. "As far as the government is concerned, this is an Indian problem. And a Papagos Indian problem, which makes it even less important to Washington. The Papagos, to put it mildly, got fleeced years ago. Their lands have been systematically stripped away from them. Papagos, as you know, means "bean people." They don't like to call themselves that. They call themselves "The People," Tohono O'otam. They're peaceful, weavers and farmers. They've never been on the warpath, as far as I know. That's why I find it hard to believe what this

Kohono-si told you. The Papagos would never rise up. I've got someone out looking for this Kohono-si now. And as for this eagle business — " Murphy shrugged.

"You don't believe it?" Thomas asked.

"It's not a matter of believing, Mr. Mullin. The Papagos believe all kinds of things. They believe the earth is alive. They believe the sun and moon are alive, that plants and animals can talk." Murphy took a deep breath. "This eagle thing has always been part of their culture. The eagle is something like their head god. He flies highest, he lives on the highest peak, he sees all, that kind of thing. To tell you the truth, I've had reports out of the Papagos reservation for a while now about deaths from some sort of eagle, but even when I tried to find out what was going on on my own, the Papagos wouldn't talk to me. There was a reservation man out there from Washington a couple of months ago, and he found out nothing either. Not that he tried. The point is, it's their own business."

"Even if someone's murdering people?"

"Frankly, yes." Murphy stretched up tall; his red hair nearly brushed the ceiling. "It's their own business. They have a council of old men, and what they call a Keeper of the Smoke. These people believe dreams control their lives and destinies. And unless they specifically asked for my help, they can't have it."

"All right," Thomas said. His face had a determined look.

"Now hold on," Murphy said. "I know what you've got in mind, and I'm going to help you all I can. Your friend Adams here told me all about that bulldog streak in you. I just want to lay down some ground rules."

"You honestly don't believe Bill Adams was murdered?"

Again Murphy stretched up, sighed. "No. I believe he went up there looking for his daughter, and that he sat with the council, and that the Keeper of the Smoke gave him peyote, and that he drank himself to death. You heard Dr. Leonard upstairs say it could happen."

"*Could* happen."

Murphy looked frustrated. His hand brushed the table on which the autopsied body of Bill Adams lay, and he pulled his hand away. "*Did* happen. You were here, you heard the doctor, you saw him sign the death certificate. Leonard knows his stuff, he's seen this happen a few times before, to Papagos."

"And Tahini?"

"Tahini was murdered. But like I said, it's none of our business. Even if Bill Adams murdered him, which I don't think happened."

79

"Someone murdered him, Marshal, and logic tells me that someone murdered Bill Adams, too."

Murphy said nothing for a moment, then said, "I'll do all I can from my end, Mr. Mullin. *If* you agree to my ground rules. I want you to let me know what you're up to. I'm going to give you a letter of introduction in case you need it. It'll legitimize you, especially with some of the white people around here. I don't want you to go out to the Papagos reservation alone. There's a man here I trust, he'll go with you. And I want you to promise not to stir up a hornets' nest out there. I've got my hands full with the President coming. Find Adams's daughter if you want to. And . . ." Murphy paused.

"Yes, Marshal?" Thomas asked.

Murphy looked at the back wall. "If you find out Adams was murdered after all, let me handle it."

Thomas held out his hand, and Murphy took it.

"Done," Thomas said.

Chapter Ten

The man Murphy had picked to go with them turned out to be a half-breed named Bartow. He was short, wiry, and unshaved; and besides his constant talking, and an annoying preference for beef jerky, which he gnawed on insistently, he seemed to have no bad habits. Whenever he smiled, which was often, he showed brown teeth, with a few obvious gaps.

"Never did know a full-breed with half a lick of sense," he said, spitting. They were already an hour out of Tucson, which receded into a pleasant bowl-like haze behind them. "You take your normal Tohono O'otam, he'll sit in the sun with his eyes closed all day, dreaming of nothing. His crops'll fail, the rain could come and beat down on his head, he'll just stay on sittin'. My mammy tol' me these people were fruity, and I believed my mammy. Even before they had likker, they were crazy people. Few times I saw my daddy that's what he was doin', sitting out there in the sun and rain."

Bartow smiled, put his jerky in his mouth and tore off a chew. "Yep — "

"That'll be enough," Thomas said. "You think maybe you'd like to scout on ahead, find us a good place to camp tonight?"

"Hell, that place you tol' me about afore sounds good enough to me. 'Circle of the Saguaro,' they call it here. Don't you like it no more?"

Thomas sighed. "How about going on *past* it, finding us another place? This way we can ride into the reservation tomorrow, early."

Bartow considered for a short moment. "Heck, if you want, chief. I could do that." He smiled again, tore off another bite of jerky.

With relief, Thomas said, "Please."

Bartow smiled, kicked his horse, and rode ahead.

"Whew!" Lincoln Reeves said, when the man was out of earshot. "I thought he'd never be quiet."

"He never would have. I knew a man like him at Fort Davis, before you were there. Bill Adams called him Gummy, since he was always moving his gums. From Louisiana, old slave family. I think his folks put him in the Army so they wouldn't have to listen to him anymore."

Lincoln grinned.

The older man turned to him. "So what are your thoughts about all this, Trooper?"

"Well," Reeves said, "I think the Papagos

are in the middle of something bad, and those white folks back in Tucson either don't care or don't know how bad it can be."

Thomas nodded solemnly. "That's very good thinking. Have you imagined what it would be like if there was an Indian war out here now?"

"I don't want to, Lieutenant."

Thomas was about to scold the young man for calling him by his Army title, but decided he didn't mind it so much. Maybe he was getting soft and old, after all. "Let me paint a picture for you, then. They'd be totally unprepared. The nearest Army garrison is ten days' ride. There are still enough Apaches in the mountains out here, and still enough of them that remember Pretorio and Victorio before him, that there'd be a lot of blood on the ground before it was over. These white people out here think the Indian Wars are over. I don't know if they'll ever be over, until Washington has finally succeeded in destroying all the culture these people have. If the Papagos rise with the Apaches to fight, and have a strong leader, I think they could go on into Tucson itself."

Reeves whistled.

"Can you imagine that, Trooper?" Thomas said. "Can you imagine that fine new city, with its wide streets, cathedrals, and university, trying to fend off an Indian raid with its police force and whatever shopkeepers Marshal Murphy could get together? These white people are babies, Trooper. There'd be blood everywhere. The fact that the Army would crush the Apaches once they got here is irrelevant. There would be a lot of damage in those few days between the telegram going out and the garrison arriving."

"Why didn't you tell Murphy this?"

"Because he wouldn't have believed me. I was playing a game back there, Trooper. Murphy is a good man, but he's a white man and as a white man he could only let me go so far in trusting me. He wouldn't want a Negro telling him his business, no matter how good a man he is. He has the force of a dominant culture behind him. Let's be cold about it, Trooper. Do you think if Bill Adams hadn't been white, the marshal would have let us come out here to risk our hides to find his killer?"

Lincoln was silent.

"Do you?" Thomas pursued.

Lincoln said, "Back home, my farm isn't my own. There's a white man in Birmingham who owns the land, the horses, the house, everything. He owns half of what I produce. Sometimes, Lieutenant, I think the Emanci-

84

pation Proclamation and the Thirteenth Amendment are just pieces of paper."

Thomas laughed grimly. "They are, Trooper. When I got out of the Army I saw just how true that is. We have to be very careful in this world. Do you remember what I once told you, what my friend Ames in the War Between the States told me? 'Hold what you have very tight, and it will not get away.' Do you remember what happened to Ames, Trooper?"

Lincoln was silent.

"You remember all right," Thomas said. "His white captain kept sending him out on the worst missions, until a bullet finally found him." Thomas was about as angry as Reeves had ever seen him. "That's us, Trooper. We always get the worst missions."

They caught up with Bartow late in the afternoon. To their surprise, the half-breed had already set up a comfortable camp, and was lounging with his bedroll rolled at his back against a rock, chewing at a huge piece of jerky. Thomas found himself liking this man, despite his bad habits. Though he said he had never been in the Army, he had Army written all over him. He was disciplined and neat. Thomas liked that.

If only he could cut out the man's tongue . . .

"Howdy, boys!" Bartow said in greeting. "Been waiting on you for hours. Hungry?"

Thomas began to say no, fearing the man would hold out his ragged jerky, but instead Bartow got up and went over to a robustly smoldering fire. Over it, on a stick spit, was a roasting piece of meat.

"What is that?" Lincoln asked.

Bartow smiled. "What do you think?"

Lincoln examined the small carcass. "Rabbit?"

Bartow laughed. "Heck, no! Ain't no rabbits out here!" He turned to Thomas. "Care to guess, chief?"

"It's prairie dog," Thomas said simply. The lines of the cooking body were unmistakable.

"Yep!" Bartow laughed.

Lincoln made a face. "Can't remember ever eating prairie dog . . ."

Bartow said, "Tasty as anything! Tried for a snake, but couldn't catch one of the critters. Maybe tonight . . ." He turned to the prairie dog carcass, humming to himself, and turned it on the spit.

Lincoln made another face at Thomas who shrugged.

"When in Rome . . ." Thomas said.

Lincoln continued to grimace.

But the meal was good, and Lincoln found himself licking the bones on his plate, and wishing there were more.

He was about to tell this to Thomas, but when he opened his mouth to speak, Thomas held a hand up to quiet him. The Lieutenant was watching Bartow with concentration while the half-breed arranged the bones on his own tin plate in a meticulously careful fashion.

Finally, Thomas said, "What are you doing?"

Bartow looked up, smiled. "Nothing, chief. Just a little precaution is all. Something my daddy told me about, a long time ago. Reading the bones. Injun thing."

"Bartow, do you know anything about an eagle on Kitt Peak?"

Bartow looked up quickly. His eyes clouded over momentarily, then he smiled. "Hell, no, chief."

"Nothing about young girls being killed?"

Bartow shook his head, keeping his smile. "Like I tol' you, no, chief."

Thomas continued to watch as the scout held two slivers of bone up above his plate and let them fall. The man's face clouded over as they landed.

Suddenly Bartow flipped his plate into the fire, watching the bones scatter.

"What did they say?" Reeves asked, while Thomas looked intently on.

"Nothing at all," Bartow said. His demeanor had changed, and he no longer smiled.

"Something, I think," Thomas said.

Bartow waved a hand in dismissal, rose, and pushed out his bedroll next to the fire.

"What did they say?" Lincoln asked again.

Bartow lay down with his back to them.

"Only something 'bout death," he said, and said no more.

The next day dawned clean and dry. The sky was as high and blue as any Thomas had ever seen in West Texas. Bartow was already packed and ready to ride, though Lincoln was just stretching out of his own bedroll. The fire, Thomas saw, had gone out, leaving a bed of ashes. If they wanted coffee, they would have to start a new one.

Bartow said, "We should get moving."

"Why?" Thomas said. If he didn't have his coffee, and if he didn't shave, he would not feel as if the day had started.

Bartow shrugged nervously. "Just should."

"What's eating at you, Bartow?" Lincoln said.

Bartow gave Reeves a solemn look. "Nothing. Just think we should get on with it."

Thomas packed his bedroll, and, as Lincoln

88

bent to tend to the fire, he prepared his shaving kit. "We'll leave soon enough. Get down and have coffee with us."

Bartow took a sliver of jerky from his pocket and tore at it unenthusiastically. "Think I'll ride a little ahead."

Thomas looked at him. "Suit yourself. But don't ride on more than an hour ahead."

Bartow nodded grimly and set off.

"What's eating him?" Lincoln said.

"He's superstitious," Thomas said. "But now we have to make sure that his foolishness doesn't get in the way of what we have to do."

In his mind, Thomas cursed Marshal Murphy lightly for burdening him with this extra problem.

An hour later, Thomas and Reeves were ready to ride. Thomas felt ready for the day now; his clothes, which had been neatly folded the night before, had been put on in military order, and his belly was full. His face was shaved.

With some annoyance, he had noticed that domestic life had put a little slack in Lincoln Reeves. But he was mildly critical to the Trooper, thinking back on his own creeping slovenliness back in Boston.

"Do you miss the Army, Trooper?" he

asked Reeve as they set out.

Lincoln pondered the question. "Can't say I do."

"Are you sure? Wasn't there a telegram you were supposed to send home?"

"Damn!" Lincoln swore. Back in Tucson, he had promised himself to send the telegram, and then forgotten again. "She'll kill me, Matty will."

"I doubt that," Thomas said. "But she will be worried. That's why I sent it for you."

Lincoln beamed. "Thank you, sir."

"Told her you missed her terribly."

"I do!" Reeve protested.

"I'm sure you do, Trooper. But I'm also sure you miss this life, just as I do."

Again, Lincoln pondered. "To be truthful, I do. But a farmer is what I am now, sir. And when this is over, I'll go back to farming."

Thomas smiled. "I told her that too, Trooper."

When they hadn't caught up with Bartow after an hour and a half, Thomas began to worry. But then they saw the half-breed, waiting for them at the top of a rise. As they got closer they saw him sitting in his saddle, pulling on a piece of jerky, solemnly watching them approach.

"I been thinking, chief," he said to Thomas.

"Yes?"

"Well, I'm going to have to leave after tonight. I got business back in Tucson to take care of."

"You'll take us into the reservation?"

Bartow sat up taller in his saddle. "I promised to do that, and I will. But tonight I'm leaving."

"Fair enough. But I want you to tell Murphy what you did."

Bartow chewed his jerky thoughtfully. "He won't be happy."

"That's not my problem, Bartow."

Bartow nodded. "Reckon it's my problem, then, chief. I'll do it."

Bartow turned, and Thomas and Lincoln followed.

They reached the reservation two hours later. It spread out below them in the cradle of two mountains. One of them, the taller, Thomas took for Kitt Peak. He noted that Bartow shied away from it, taking them far to the west, approaching from the base of the other mountain.

Thomas had been in many Indian reservations, but he had never seen one quite as depressed as this one. These were a beaten people. There were more wooden shacks than teepees; outside many were naked, dirty children playing in the dust. Down the middle of what served as their main road, a ditch filled with foul-looking water ran. Saguaro cactus grew here and there. Outside the few teepees, old women sat weaving baskets. Their clothing was a mixture of traditional and the white man's, scarves and dirty dresses. No one smiled.

It was a large reservation, and they rode for fifteen minutes before reaching their destination, a large wooden building with a sagging, shingled roof. On its porch, every other plank seemed to be missing. The word OFFICE had faded, though someone had recently whitewashed the word COUNCIL in crooked letters above it.

Inside, the accommodations were no better than what they had seen. A table missing one leg, supported by fruit cases, stood just inside the door. On top of it were scattered papers, some with United States government markings on them. Thomas picked one up. It was a newsletter, from Washington, talking about new programs for education, housing, and the distribution of clothing and foodstuffs. It was a year old, and the more Thomas read, the more he saw how evasive and complicated it was. Nothing had been promised before 1905, and only if a myriad of forms were filled out and properly filed.

Thomas put the paper down.

Along the back of the room was a counter. Behind that, mostly empty shelves held a few blankets and a lot of cooking utensils. More boxes of cooking utensils stood open on the floor in front of the counter.

A few other tables, missing one or two legs and supported by empty boxes or crates, were scattered around the room. A few old men sat at them, staring into space. Along the far right wall were a few cots; on one of them, a figure lay curled, uncovered, face to the wall, eyes open.

There was a back room. An old man came out of it to wait at the counter for them. There was some sort of recognition between the old man and Bartow; when the old man raised his hand listlessly, though, Bartow said nothing.

"Here for more jerky?" the old man asked thickly, offering a tired smile. His eyes, half-vacant, turned on Lincoln and Thomas.

Bartow said, "Marshal Murphy sent me with these two. They're looking for Bill Adams's daughter."

The old man's eyes went to stone.

"You heard about Adams and Tahini?" Bartow offered.

"We heard. They're burying Tahini down

93

in the city, the mining company's taking care of it. We said fine. We have our own burial today."

Bartow's interest was heightened he chewed on his own jerky faster. "Who?"

"Kohono-si. He was cut up like Tahini." The old man waited for Bartow's reaction.

Bartow said, "I threw the bones last night."

"So," the old man said. Then he added, "You belong here with us."

Unaccountably, Bartow smiled, showing his teeth. In a moment, he seemed to have returned to his old self.

"Be damned if I do!"

"That's no way to speak of the dead."

"So what!"

The old man looked off into the distance. "You will understand some day. You cannot leave us behind. Especially not now."

"Bull-spit." Bartow heaved a sigh of relief, and turned to Thomas and Lincoln with his smile intact. "Let's go about our business, chief," he said to Thomas. "I can stay with you now."

The old man frowned.

"Le-Cato in?" Bartow asked the old man.

"The Keeper of the Smoke is at his home, preparing for a trip."

"Fine." Bartow turned to leave, then came back to the counter.

"Think I will have some of that jerky, if you don't mind!"

Frowning still, the old man sold him what he wanted, and they left.

"Got to understand," Bartow said to Thomas as they mounted and rode slowly to the edge of the village, "I thought I was a dead man until five minutes ago. This bone thing always works for me. The rest of it" — he waved his hand — "is bull-spit. But that bone thing worked the night my daddy died, and the night my momma died. And now . . ."

"I take it you're not close to your tribe?" Thomas said.

Bartow laughed. "Not likely, chief. I went to Tucson. Never really cared for it."

"But that's not the way Abby Adams felt? Is that why she came back here?"

"Couldn't say," Bartow replied. His face clouded momentarily.

Thomas said, "I think we should attend this funeral."

Bartow looked at him unhappily, then said, "If you want, chief."

The Keeper of the Smoke's house was better looking than the rest, but not by much. It looked as though at one time it had been very cozy and neat, but time, and lack of maintenance, had made the eaves sag and the front door hung at an angle. Le-Cato himself sat on the front porch in a chair, out of the sun, staring at the street. Nearby, his horse was being packed by a young squaw, who ignored them.

"Hey, old man!" Bartow called.

Le-Cato looked at them, startled. "You are a dream," he rasped.

"Hell, no, Le-Cato, we ain't no dream! Got to talk to you, is all."

The old man had regained his bearings, and sat staring at Thomas.

"Yes," he said, "we will talk." He turned to the young squaw. "Granddaughter, leave us."

Without looking at them, the young girl stopped what she was doing and walked away.

But after a long talk with the Keeper of the Smoke, Thomas felt as though he had learned nothing, except for the fact that the old man had nothing to say to him. He spoke in circles. But despite all that, Thomas felt the man's keen interest in him. Thomas learned nothing of Bill Adams's daughter, and nothing about the eagle, but the old man more than once put his thin hand on Thomas's knee, as if testing to see if he was real.

96

When they left, the old man seemed much happier than he had been when they arrived, and as they stepped from his porch he once again reached out to touch Thomas.

"You see that?" Bartow said with a laugh as they rode off. "Ol' Le-Cato thinks you're a dream come true!"

The funeral of Kohono-si was short and nearly devoid of ceremony. The man's body was carried down the main street of the village on a litter, and laid on the ground in front of the council store. The Keeper of the Smoke chanted a prayer, and then the litter was lifted again, to be carried outside the village limits and buried.

"I'd like to examine that body," Thomas said.

"Sure thing, chief!" Bartow said. He stepped forward, told the litter carriers to lower the body, which they did. There was a murmur from the Tohono O'otam until the Keeper of the Smoke said, "It is all right."

Thomas stepped quickly forward and looked the body over. It had, indeed, been mangled in a fashion similar to that of Tahini. This time the killing wound was a gash across the chest, at heart level. Again there were slashes on the hands and arms, as if the man had tried to ward off his attacker.

Thomas backed away, and the litter carriers bore the body away.

"Okay if we leave now, chief?" Bartow said. Through the entire ceremony he had stood smiling, chewing on his jerky.

"Yes," Thomas said.

They camped outside the village, but still in reservation territory. Bartow was no longer afraid of Kitt Peak. It loomed behind them. Just before sundown Bartow left, and returned with another prairie dog, which Lincoln looked forward to ravenously.

By the time they ate it was late, and after the long day Thomas and Lincoln turned in. They left Bartow sitting by the fire, humming, still talking as he finished his own meal.

In the middle of the night, Thomas awoke. The fire was low, but still lit. Something was wrong. He counted the outline of horses.

There were only two.

He rose and walked to where Lincoln lay sleeping. Bartow was nowhere to be seen. His bedroll had been packed; his horse was gone.

By the fire, Thomas found Bartow's plate, with a scatter of animal bones on it. They were in the same pattern they had been when Bartow had gotten so upset the night before.

"Trooper Reeves!" Thomas called. He

didn't wait for Lincoln to scramble out of sleep before setting off himself into the darkness, gun drawn.

They found Bartow two hours later. He had been heading back to Tucson; his horse stood near his body, huffing impatiently, and waiting to be led. Bartow was face up, staring at the stars, head thrown back. As they got closer, Thomas could see the pulled back rictal look of fear on the man's face.

"That's the way Sergeant Adams looked," Reeves said.

"Yes," Thomas said. He examined the body. There were marks of a struggle, claw marks on the arms and hands. Thomas crawled close to Bartow's face, brought his nose down to the dead man's mouth, and sniffed.

"Lieutenant — " Lincoln said in distaste.

"Quiet, Trooper." He continued to sniff, then, to Lincoln's disbelief, put his finger into Bartow's mouth and scraped against his teeth. He then brought the finger close to his nose and sniffed.

"All right," Thomas said, getting up. He strode back to his horse, pulled his bedroll down, and rolled it out.

"You take the first watch, Trooper," he said to Reeves, then promptly lay down, and rolled himself up.

Shaking his head at Thomas's antics, Lincoln unslung his rifle, crouched in the shadows near the newly made camp, and looked to the stars for four hours before Thomas Mullin awoke, alert and bright-eyed, to take his place.

Chapter Eleven

With pride, Lone Wolf watched as a representative of the last of the Six Tribes approached his camp. The rider halted below, looked up, and held his staff of feathers high overhead in greeting. In answer, Lone Wolf raised his hand high in salute.

Lowering his staff, the rider continued to climb his horse up the steep path to the top of the bluff.

Content, Lone Wolf turned back to the Council. The other members had been fed, and were now smoking. Curling Smoke was telling a story to keep them amused. Lone Wolf had grudging admiration for the old man; Curling Smoke had, at least according to himself, been in nearly every major war party of the past fifty years, including the last one of Geronimo. According to Curling Smoke, Geronimo had been a good chief who had merely grown too tired to fight, and now allowed himself to be shown in circuses and newspaper photos. Once that had happened, Curling Smoke said, some of the greatness had bled out of Geronimo, like the blood from a slain deer. Curling Smoke and Geronimo were nearly the same age, and still Curling Smoke fought on. The implication was clear.

Lone Wolf half-listened to the old man's rambling story about a raid on a fort while he waited impatiently for the new emissary to arrive. This day would prove him triumphant as a chief. No one had been able to call a war council in nearly five years. The white man's reservations were full and seemingly secure. Only up north, in what the white men referred to as Canada, were any war parties, and small ones at that, operating anymore.

It was as if the Apache tribes had given birth only to women, fit to do women's work.

But all that might change. Lone Wolf was no fool. He had studied the campaigns of Geromino and of Victorio, and, most recently, Pretorio. They had all failed for one reason alone. The white man's army had been close by, and great in numbers. With white man's schooling in the reservation, Lone Wolf had learned how to read maps and books. His teachers did not notice that the only books and maps he was really interested in were concerned with the so-called Indian Wars. He had studied well, and began to form his own plan when he was fifteen.

That was five years ago, just as Pretorio

was being quickly beaten and sent back to his reservation in New Mexico. Those had been bad times for the Apache. Throughout all the tribes, an unspoken feeling of defeat had descended. The white man seemed to sense this, and his iron grip had relaxed. The forts to the west had been strengthened, and those here in Arizona, and east into New Mexico and Texas had been weakened. Fort Davis, in Texas, which Pretorio had attempted to attack, had been closed, and the dreaded Buffalo Soldiers dispersed. All along the middle West, the white man had relaxed, secure in his telegraph lines, his federal marshals, his farmers, his towns of merchants and shopkeepers.

This Lone Wolf had waited for. Patiently, and with the outward appearance of docility, he had learned and waited for this moment.

And now there would be great war again.

But this time it would be different. For Lone Wolf would win. He would not fight a war of numbers, but of stealth. Conquest would be foolish. Lone Wolf was well aware of the might of the United States of America, and knew that any attack on those farmers, or shopkeepers, or the white man's precious railroad would bring swift and terrible retribution. Lone Wolf would not be a flaming sword in the side of the United States, but rather a sharp thorn. He would not fight the Army. He would, instead, strike one terrible blow, one sharp thrust of the thorn, that would at once hurt the white race mightily and provide a rallying point for *all* the Indian tribes from west to east. And soon he, Lone Wolf, would be the greatest chief of them all, rallying a hundred thousand braves throughout all of the United States, a force too mighty for the white man's army to conquer.

Perhaps an alliance with Mexico, or Spain, would follow. The United States would reel from the blow the mighty Lone Wolf would strike.

If only the final piece of his plan would fall into place . . .

"And the white men cowered behind their wagons," Curling Smoke was saying behind him, "and waited for their deaths to come. And come they did." Lone Wolf turned to see Curling Smoke address White Deer, the representative of the Mescalero tribe, and Pretorio's only descendent. "And you will enjoy this, White Deer. For when we went in later to take scalps, the three soldiers who had been accompanying the caravan were Buffalo Soldiers, their black faces twisted in painful death."

White Deer nodded.

Lone Wolf turned back to face the valley

below as the new representative topped the rise.

For a moment, all was silent. Lone Wolf knew the Council behind him was watching him, waiting for his reaction. This was a pivotal time. The new representative halted his horse, and looked at Lone Wolf. Lone Wolf stared back hard.

Suddenly, Lone Wolf raised his hands in greeting.

"Welcome, brother."

At first reluctant, the new representative breathed deeply and raised his feather stick in greeting.

"Thank you, brother," the new one said. "I bring greetings from the Tohono O'otam, who have sent me here as their representative. The eagle has flown high, in many dreams, and has told us that this is what we must do."

The rider dismounted, and Lone Wolf strode forward, and embraced him.

"It is good that you have come, Le-Cato. It is good that the Keeper of the Smoke of the Tohono O'otam has brought his people into this great undertaking."

The old man stiffened, then embraced Lone Wolf.

"The eagle has told us to make it so," he said, with sadness, and suddenly the embrace was a genuine one.

Chapter Twelve

Lincoln woke up groggy the next morning. For a moment he didn't know where he was, and called out to Matty to make breakfast, because he couldn't smell her coffee as he usually did. He wondered if little Washington was outside playing, because his son usually came to wake him up if he overslept. There were chores to be done, seed to plant —

"Get up, Trooper," Thomas Mullin's voice said. Now Lincoln knew where he was. He groaned. A large part of him wished he was back in Birmingham, getting ready for a normal day with his family.

Lincoln rose up on his elbows. Lieutenant Mullin was bent over a small fire near the body of Bartow. For a moment, Lincoln thought the old man was building a funeral pyre for the half-breed, but Thomas was actually ignoring the body, and had a leather kit bag open, tiny instruments spread carefully on the flap. The Lieutenant was holding a glass tube, examining it carefully, swirling the yellowish contents around as he held it out over the small flame.

"Wha— "

"Be quiet, please, Trooper," Lieutenant Mullin said patiently. The man's eyes were glued to the glass tube. The liquid within was growing clearer, losing its yellowish tint.

"Hmm," Thomas said, and suddenly he lost all interest in the glass tube, dumped its contents out into the fire, cleaned the tube, and stored it away with its instruments.

"What was that, sir?" Lincoln asked.

"A reagent kit," Thomas replied, tucking the leather kit into his saddlebag. "I was doing something I should have done two days ago, after we examined Bill Adams's body. A crude Marsh test. It was foolish of me to take that doctor's word, though I'm sure it wasn't his fault."

"What wasn't his fault?"

"Hmm?" Thomas looked as though he had been thinking. "Nothing, Trooper. Nothing we can do anything about now, at least." He pulled his mess kit from his saddlebag, drew out coffee and biscuits. "Hungry?"

"Yes," Reeves said. "But can't you tell me — "

"Later, Trooper," Thomas said.

They ate, packed, then buried Bartow's body. Thomas marked the shallow grave, so that Marshal Murphy would be able to find it, then tied Bartow's horse behind his own. Bartow's saddlebags were filled with beef jerky and little else. Thomas held a piece out to Lincoln. "Care for a chew?"

Lincoln made a face. "No."

Thomas shrugged, pulled a strip for himself, and mounted his horse.

"Where to, Lieutenant?" Lincoln asked.

Thomas looked at the young man, as if surprised he had asked the question. "We have to visit a mining company," he said, staving off any further questions by reining his horse around and setting off at a fast pace.

Chapter Thirteen

Half Moon.

Again, the eagle awaited. Below, the long trek up to the eagle's promontory had begun, and already the eagle could hear the wails and moans of those coming. The eagle could not yet make out the girl to be sacrificed, but had no doubt that the sacrifice had been brought. The Tohono O'otam would not dare to ignore the eagle's demands.

The night was dark, deep, and high. A good night for flying. The eagle imagined soaring above the clouds on this night, touching the stars, brushing the robes of the god of heaven. The wind against the eagle's face would be cold and bracing, and the power in the eagle's wings would course throughout its body, making it quiver with strength —

"God of the sky and clouds, we have come."

The voice was different; in the near darkness, the eagle could not make out the face, but this was not the Keeper of the Smoke.

The eagle raised its wings, let them flutter down.

"Le-Cato, the Keeper of the Smoke, is not

here," the voice said. "He has gone to the Council of the Tribes, as you commanded." The voice trembled. "He has gone to make the war bond you wished."

So! This was what the eagle had wanted, and it had come true.

"We hope you are pleased," the trembling voice continued. The eagle could now make out the bowed head of Leaping Deer, one of the council members of the Tohono O'otam.

The eagle waited silently.

Leaping Deer turned to the group of wailing women behind him and drew a slight figure out. It was a young girl, no more than twelve or thirteen. She stood shaking, eyes wide, staring at the eagle.

"Great bird," Leaping Deer said, "I pray to you. This is my daughter, who has been chosen to be with you." The man's trembling voice broke. "I beseech you! Do not take her. Your wishes have been granted. Have you not promised that the sacrifices will end when you have what you want? Soon you will have it!"

When the eagle was silent, Leaping Deer shouted, "She is all I have! Do not take her from me, I will do your bidding for a thousand days and a thousand more!"

The eagle fluttered its wings, let them fall.

The wailing women wailed louder, moved

back, leaving Leaping Deer and his daughter alone.

"No!" Leaping Deer shouted, as the eagle raised its wings to strike. The council member drew his shaking daughter to him, turned, and began to make his way hurriedly down the mountain path after the old women.

The eagle rose over Leaping Deer and his daughter, and dropped upon them.

"No!" Leaping Deer said again.

But already the eagle's claws were upon the two of them, and the night was filled with their cries.

Chapter Fourteen

As Thomas had expected, he and Lincoln were met with animosity at the Ranger Copper Mine. The company was a veritable little town, with more provisions than the Tohono O'otam reservation they had visited. There was a sea of tents, made of tall strong canvas, staked in precise rows. A larger tent looked like a portable mess hall. There were semi-permanent structures, wooden buildings on stilts that looked as though they had been brought in, then set down. Horse-drawn wagons were everywhere; there was a railroad track down the center of the encampment with a small steamer engine pulling ore cars toward the mouth of the mine, at the foot of the mountain in the near distance. Thomas heard other mechanical sounds, and was surprised to see a horseless carriage chug by, its loudly tapping engine amazingly pulling a light cart.

Lincoln stared at the horseless carriage in amazement, then shook his head. "I've read about those, Lieutenant, but I've got to say, after seeing one, I don't think it'll come to much."

"Oh? Why not, Trooper?"

Reeves pointed. "Just look at it! Can hardly pull its own weight!"

"You couldn't be more wrong," Thomas said. "In a few years, that horse under your hind end will be used for nothing but recreation. What you're seeing is just the start of a new age."

"Well, I don't know — " Reeves began.

"You *boys* want something?" a harsh voice said behind them.

They stopped their horse, reined around to face a large, hard-looking man with a clipboard in one hand, and a hat pushed back on his head.

"We're looking for the foreman," Thomas said.

"You can talk to me."

"Are you the foreman?" Thomas asked mildly.

The man's face reddened, and he took a step forward. "I'm not used to being talked to that way by a nig— "

"That's enough, Frawley," another voice said. The new man approached, smiling. Like Frawley, he was cleanly dressed and had a hat pushed back on his head. But he was small, thin, with wire-rimmed glasses.

He looked up at Thomas and Lincoln, studying them. The smile stayed, but looked as though it might dissolve at any time. "I'm Mates. You come about a job?"

"No," Thomas said. He handed down his letter of introduction from Marshal Murphy.

The thin foreman studied the note for a moment, then frowned. He handed the piece of paper back up to Thomas.

"So?" he said. His smile had evaporated, leaving a bland look behind.

"Like to ask you about a man who worked for you, named Tahini."

"Tahini's dead," Frawley growled.

Thomas continued to look and speak mildly. "I know that." He addressed Mates. "What I'd like to know is if Tahini had access to any chemicals here."

Mates looked perplexed, and turned to Frawley for an answer. "Did he, Joe?"

Frawley snapped, "No."

"Did — " Thomas said, but Frawley turned and stalked away.

"You use arsenic here, don't you?" Thomas asked Mates.

Mates nodded, looking after Frawley. "Yes, we do. It's used to refine the lead that comes out of the reverberatory furnace as a waste product, after the copper is purified."

"Would Tahini have access to it?"

Mates turned his attention to Thomas, giving him a long look. "I don't think so. We don't let our" — he paused, smiled — "let's just say very few people have access to those chemicals. They're kept in locked drums in one of the trailer houses. Only myself and Frawley here can get at them."

"No one else?"

Mates gave Thomas another long look. "I don't think I'll discuss this anymore with you, Mr. Mullin. If Marshal Murphy wants to come out here himself, I'd be happy to talk with him. I know he's got his hands full with President Roosevelt coming on out to Tucson, so unless he can get away, I'm afraid that's all I have to say."

"Mr. Mates," Thomas said.

Mates turned to Frawley. "Get rid of them."

Frawley smiled. "Be a pleasure, Mr. Mates."

But Thomas and Lincoln had already reined their horses around, and were heading out of the encampment.

They were at the fringes of the encampment when a familiar voice rang out behind them.

"Glory in hell! If it ain't the darkie brothers!"

Thomas turned in his saddle.

"That's right," Samuel Forsen said. "It's me." He glared up at Thomas, his white, craggy face older, more crevassed. "Your old army friend. Remember that beating you gave me back at Fort Davis years ago?"

"When you were Captain Seavers' toady?" Thomas said.

Forsen said angrily, "That's right, darkie. You know they drummed me out after Seavers got booted back to Washington?"

"That wasn't my doing," Thomas said.

"Might as well have been," Forsen continued angrily. "Grierson knew about the fight, and did nothing about it."

"You had it coming."

Anger flared on Forsen's face, then he brought it under control with a malicious smile. "Hear your friend Adams went over the falls. Hear his daughter went Injun, too."

Thomas was silent.

"Too bad about Adams," Forsen continued. "Though I bet you wouldn't have thought as highly of him if you'd known what he was involved in. Not such a saint after all, eh?"

"What do you mean by that?" Thomas asked.

Forsen shrugged, his wicked smile widening. "Guess there's a lot you don't know, darkie. And I'd watch your back while you're around here. Could get something sharp planted in it. Can't say I'd cry at your funeral."

Forsen laughed, turned, walked away.

"Lieutenant, he can't talk to you like that," Lincoln said, starting to get down off his horse. Thomas reached over, restraining him.

"Let him go," he said.

But as Forsen sauntered away, Thomas stared after him, a pensive look on his face.

Thomas made their camp a mile away from the Ranger Copper Mine, just over a short range of hills out of sight of the company encampment. After tying the horses out of the sun, he set himself up in a hollow of rocks overlooking the mine and sat looking.

"What are you waiting for, sir?" Lincoln asked.

"Patience, Trooper," Thomas said. "I'm waiting for a reaction."

"Sir?"

"Patience," Thomas repeated.

Thomas lay down with his head in the shade of a rock overhang, crossed his arms, and closed his eyes.

"Patience and sleep are the same things to me, sir," he said.

Thomas didn't look at him, but continued to study the mining camp.

What seemed like a long time later, Lincoln was being roused from sleep. When he opened his eyes, he saw that indeed it was night. He could barely see Lieutenant Mullin's face hanging over his own.

"Get up," Thomas whispered urgently, "and be *quiet*."

Lincoln rose.

Their horses were ready to ride, and Lincoln followed Thomas's lead, and climbed into his saddle. They made their way soundlessly down the path to the plain below.

Lincoln was awake now. Straining his eyes, he saw nothing in the half-moon lit landscape below them. The Ranger Copper Mine was behind them, to their left.

They rode slowly, unspeaking, for two hours, passing between two low peaks. Still, Lincoln saw nothing ahead.

Then, an hour later, as they broke out onto a flat plain heading up between two more peaks, Lincoln spotted a lone figure riding in front of them. It was about a mile ahead, dressed in dark clothing, slouched down in the saddle.

Lincoln whispered, "Is that — ?"

Thomas motioned urgently for him to be quiet.

They rode on.

A half hour later found them within a half-mile of the riding man.

Suddenly the figure sat up alertly in the saddle, looked back, and kicked his horse into a gallop. They heard a shout of "Go, dammit!"

Thomas sat up and shouted, "Come on, Trooper!"

Lincoln kicked into his own horse and whooped, "Aren't you going to say, 'The game's afoot, sir?' "

"Ha!" Thomas shouted, as they bore down on the riding figure.

What followed was a wild midnight chase. The rider knew the low peaks and valleys, and tore through them with abandon, riding close to rock walls and stands of brush. They could hear the rider shouting, "Come on! Come on!" to his mount, which responded with speed in the darkness.

Thomas and Lincoln kept up as best they could. Lincoln began to be frightened by Thomas's headlong flight. The Lieutenant's eyes were wild with the chase, his attention riveted on the riding figure in front of them.

They broke out onto a flat plain, and Thomas and Lincoln began to gain. They could hear the horse in front of them straining, its rider exhorting it, slapping it. But the horse was tired and began to lose speed.

"We've got him!" Thomas cried, exultantly.

But suddenly they brushed a low hill, and the rider in front veered left around its curve. Thomas and Lincoln blindly followed.

Before they knew it, they found themselves

in a field of saguaro cactus, the massive tall arms reaching out at them in the dark. . . .

As Thomas ducked under a curving arm, he heard Lincoln cry out just behind him and turned to see the Trooper go down, his horse rearing as Reeves was knocked off.

In front of him, the rider wove back and forth, and now broke out of the field, climbed a short rise, and was gone.

"Damn!" Thomas cried.

In the lengthening distance he heard the escaping rider whoop a laugh.

Thomas turned his mount and went back to Lincoln, who lay moaning on the ground, holding his leg.

The young man looked up sheepishly, restraining a groan.

"Sorry, sir."

Thomas dismounted. Lincoln was momentarily frightened by the anger on the older man's face, fearing it was directed at him.

"Sir, I'm sor— "

"Be quiet, Trooper," Thomas snapped. "He would have gotten away, anyway. I'm mad at myself for following him in here." He stared angrily in the direction the rider had gone. Turning back to help Lincoln up, he balled his fists. The anger hadn't left his face.

"That man, whoever he is, knows everything."

Chapter Fifteen

Barty Smith was doing what he liked to do best. He was in his favorite part of Arizona, with a pack full of traded goods from Mexico, a fully belly, a moon overhead to read his paper by, and all the alone he wanted.

The paper was nearly new, only three weeks old. The wily old Mexican, Romulez, had thrown it into the deal at the last minute, hoping to sweeten the pot. Barty had nearly snapped at the bait, but his dealer's instinct had held him back, making him yawn.

"Papers from th' East don't do much for me no more, Romulez," he'd said.

Romulez had pretended to look crestfallen. "But my friend, I brought it back just for you from Kansas City. It has all the news of *Washington* in it. Haven't you always bragged about how you were born in Washington, the cradle of democracy, as you call it? Haven't you always been hungry for news of this town? Look," Romulez said, holding the newspaper under Barty's nose. "It is the *New York Times!*"

Barty yawned again. "Maybe you can use

it to wallpaper your hacienda, Romulez. . . ."

They had played their game for another ten minutes, until Barty had finally closed the deal at a few pennies more, which was all Romulez was after. They both went away happy. And now Barty, born Bartholomew Carson Smith, to a rich banker in Washington, D.C., indeed could indulge in his favorite thing, which was to read up on the news of his long-lost and little-lamented first home, the nation's capital.

He saw that Theodore Roosevelt himself was on his campaign swing west and would stop in Arizona, Tucson, of all places, to make a speech —

A night noise, louder than it should be, startled Barty out of lowering his newspaper away from the firelight.

"What the hell — "

There, sitting tall above him, was something that must be an illusion, an Apache in the saddle, bare-breasted, rifle in hand.

"Hey, chief," Barty laughed, "anyone tell you the Indian Wars ended years ago?"

Behind the solemn rider were five more Apaches, similarly painted.

The brave asked curtly, "Are you an Army scout?"

Barty, not liking the Indian's tone, said abruptly, "Ain't no Army for three hundred miles of here. Now, chief," Barty said, starting to get up. "I don't know what your game is, but the reservation is that-a-way — "

As he rose, holding the paper in front of him, the Apache brave fired his rifle, blowing a hole in the front page of *The New York Times* and through Barty.

Barty shouted, disbelieving.

Another rifle shot sounded, and a third, and Barty lay silent on his back, mouth open in dying incomprehension.

The Apache brave held his rifle up in salute to his companions.

"He was alone," the brave said. "Ride back to the others. Tell them the way to Oto-A-Pe is clear."

His companions whooped, turned, and rode madly back.

The Apache paused to look down at the unmoving white man, new ragged newspaper scattering around him. Then the brave turned, whooping once himself, to ride back and join his brothers.

Chapter Sixteen

Lincoln and Thomas were emerging from the pass leading from the cactus field when three men surrounded them. Thomas didn't see faces; there were bandanas covering the features, and the men had their hats pulled down over their eyes. But he did recognize the one gruff voice that told the other two men to "be quick about it," and then told one of them to shut up when he started to mention the gruff man's name.

"Just do it," the gruff man said.

Lincoln, groaning from his hurt leg, was hauled down off his horse by one of the riders and thrown to the ground. A gun was held to his head.

"You get up, darkie, you die," the gruff voice said.

The other rider motioned Thomas down at gunpoint, and when Thomas had dismounted, the gruff one faced the Lieutenant.

"I'm gonna enjoy this," the man said. Then to the one holding Thomas at gunpoint, he added, "Hold him."

The man put his gun away and pinned

Thomas's arms behind him. Then the gruff one reached his fist back and hit Thomas square in the jaw.

Thomas's head twisted to one side, then he looked the gruff one straight in the eye and said, "Why don't you show your face? You always were a coward, Forsen."

"Damn, he knows you!" the one covering Lincoln said. "You said he wouldn't — what are we gonna do now?"

"Shut up and cover the other darkie," Forsen said. He drew down this bandana and smiled at Thomas. "I don't care if you see my face, since I'm gonna kill you, anyway."

"Hey, wait a minute!" the one covering Lincoln said. "You said we'd beat 'em up is all! I don't want no trouble from Murphy in town!"

Forsen turned on him. "I said, shut up!"

The other man took in a deep breath, but said nothing.

Forsen turned on Thomas and hit him again. This time the Lieutenant went black for a moment. When he came to, Forsen was already swinging at him again.

"You . . . always . . . were . . . a . . . coward. . . ." He got out, and then he heard his own voice fade away.

He awoke to, he thought, the sun rising.

125

But he found that when he tried to open his eyes, he could not, they were so swollen. He heard movement nearby.

"Trooper?"

"Here, Lieutenant." Lincoln sounded weak but alive.

"They beat you?"

"They were going to, but the one covering me with the gun wouldn't let them. He and Forsen had a fight. Forsen was going to shoot you after you were down. The one covering me turned his gun on him and made him back away. The third one sided against Forsen, finally, and they rode out."

"How's your leg?"

"Broken, sir." Lincoln laughed through pain.

Thomas laughed, too, but found that when he did it, his face hurt, "Lord . . ."

"Just take it easy, sir."

"What time is it?"

"Midday."

"What!"

"I thought you were dead, Lieutenant. Forsen beat you so bad I thought you'd died. But I couldn't crawl over there. . . ."

Lincoln winced in pain.

"It's all right. We'll get out of this soon. . . ."

But suddenly Thomas felt a wave of pain and weakness come over him. His limbs wouldn't respond when he tried to move them. Then blackness in the midst of day claimed him again.

When Thomas awoke again it was twilight. Now, he was able to open his eyes a little. He saw Lincoln next to him, seemingly asleep, an open canteen beside him.

"Lord, what a pair," Thomas whispered, and this time when he tried to move his arms they worked, and he sat up.

Gently, he felt his face. He didn't like the contours his fingers found. But there was nothing broken. His nose was bloodied, and his jaw ached, and his eyes hurt when he opened them to more than a squint, but the fact was that Forsen, besides being a coward, did not pack a deadly punch. For that, Thomas was gratetul.

He moved slowly to Trooper Reeves, and shook the young man awake.

"Trooper."

"Sir . . ."

"You washed my eyes, didn't you, Trooper?"

"Yes," Reeves said with some effort. "Was able to crawl on over to you. . . ."

Thomas felt the young man's forehead. There was fever. The broken leg had obviously become infected.

"Don't say another thing, Trooper," Thomas said. "We're getting out of here, now. I'm getting you to a doctor."

"Thank you, sir. . . ." Reeves said faintly.

"I said don't speak! And thank *you*, Trooper."

"It's all right, sir. . . ."

Groaning with the hurt in his body, Thomas Mullin hauled himself to his feet, staggered to the horses, and before long had pulled the now unconscious Trooper onto his horse, tethered behind Thomas's own. With a mighty effort, he pulled himself up into his own saddle, and turned toward Tucson.

After one of the longest nights he had ever spent, Thomas finally reached the city an hour before dawn. He rode on to Marshal Murphy's office. When he received no response, he tied the horses up. An overwhelming weariness overcame him. He nearly blacked out. Summoning his last reserves of strength, he brought the unconscious Lincoln off his horse and set him against the front of the Marshal's building. Then he sat down beside the young man, and closed his eyes.

"We'll just wait here awhile, Trooper," he said, trying to summon strength that wasn't there.

Once more, blackness overtook him.

128

Chapter Seventeen

They moved liked clouds on the silent wind.

Lone Wolf was proud of his braves. Even Curling Smoke, at his advanced age, had seemed to draw strength from their mission, turning into a young buck again. The only one that Lone Wolf did not fully trust was Le-Cato, the Tohono O'otam, the Papagos chief, who had not raised his hand against one of the white men they had found along their path. Even the large group of campers they had swooped down upon, with blood enough for all, had proven too small a band for Le-Cato to join in the killing. Afterward, when scalps had been taken, he and Le-Cato had locked eyes, and the old man had turned away.

In two days they would be in the land of Le-Cato's people, and then the Papagos would either prove worthy hosts, or unworthy opponents. Lone Wolf knew that the Tohono O'otam would not oppose him, if only because Le-Cato had given his word; but the unspoken understanding was that if Le-Cato's people did anything to harm their enterprise, the Tohono O'otam would be slaughtered. Even in this day of domination by the white man, the government could not prevent that. When the other tribes rose up against Le-Cato's people, the white man would come too late to the rescue. This Le-Cato and Lone Wolf both knew. So a kind of truce was maintained.

Then again, Lone Wolf had not told Le-Cato of their true mission, and what the eagle who lived on Oto-A-Pe was getting for them. If Le-Cato knew these things, he would doubtless oppose Lone Wolf, no matter what the consequences. And before Lone Wolf's plan had been carried out, he doubted he could muster any opposition against the Tohono O'otam from the other tribes. For now, he needed the old man.

Lone Wolf turned to look at Le-Cato now. "Soon we will be in the land of the eagle, brother."

Le-Cato looked at him wearily, and nodded.

"And the people of the eagle will prove a good friend of the Apache, will they not?"

Le-Cato drew himself up, still looking at Lone Wolf, and nodded curtly again.

"Good, brother," Lone Wolf said, smiling, and turned to urge his own horse ahead at a faster pace.

Two more days.

Two more days and Reney Coleman would

have the weekend off. One weekend a month, and damn if that wasn't enough.

But, working for the white man, working for the Ranger Copper Mine, you took what they gave you, smiled, and kept smiling even when they took half of it away.

Reney stretched, stepped out of his pup tent, looked at the stars. Clear night. Then, nearly every night in this damn desert was clear. Nothing like Memphis, Tennessee. Sometimes he missed Memphis, not the people but the land. There was a little more to the seasons, there. This time of year, winter would be huffing its breath, ready to leave soon. And, in another month or so, spring would start to rise. He loved spring in Tennessee, the smell of hickory trees in bloom, the flowers. Out here in godforsaken Arizona, there was spring, but it looked much like winter and fall and summer. Degrees of heat was the only difference. In spring, you wouldn't be able to stand outside at three in the afternoon without burning your tailbone off, and in winter you could. Big difference.

Reney wondered about the black man he had met on the train the week before. Now there was a fellow looking for trouble. Said he liked this part of the country, too. Negroes like that made Reney nervous. Always pushing for more. And all that usually got the pusher was the business end of a whip or rope. And this man had been tough. More than Army tough. Black stone.

Reney sighed, wished the man well. Mullin, his name had been. Probably dead by now, though you never knew . . .

Stretching again, Reney looked at his dead fire, decided it didn't need relighting, and turned to go back into his tent to sleep. Time to head out back East to the mining company tomorrow, get his pay, get into Tucson for the weekend, maybe even catch a glimpse of who's-his-name, Teddy Roosevelt —

Something caught Reney's eye, way off in the distance against the dark horizon of a hill.

He had good eyes, and turned to look that way. Nothing. But then, something. A dark shape, high on a horse, standing still. The movement of the horse's head had caught his attention.

Quiet as a mouse, Reney left his tent behind and crept to the edge of his hollow. He could still see the top of the rider above him. Reney was well hidden, and if he was quiet he was sure the other man couldn't see him. Strangers, especially at night, were not something that Reney wanted near his camp.

He crouched, slowly climbed up out of his hollow, keeping the rider's head in view until it was hidden by the rocks above.

He stopped when he reached the top of the rise, then slowly raised his head.

The rider was gone.

Damn.

He rose higher. At first he saw nothing on the sloping plain below, a stand of saguaro in the moonlight, nothing more.

Then, one of the cactus moved, and he had his rider in sight.

Injun. No doubt about it, the way the man rode, and Reney could now see the man's bare back. Reney wondered what the hell a Papagos was doing here, thirty miles from his reservation, where he was neither wanted nor allowed.

A chill went up Reney's back as he realized that the stand of saguaro the Injun had ridden into was not a field of cactus at all, but other riders.

Reney counted six — no, seven. Seven Injuns, tall in the saddle, grouped in the moonlight.

Then another chill went up Reney's back as the original Injun he had seen waved to something in the distance, and a small army of Injuns appeared out of the darkness of the far hills and rode silently toward the group of seven.

Reney lost count at eighty, and stood rooted to his spot as the small army hooked up with

133

the new band, then rode straight toward him, passing on the plain below, not fifty feet from the hollow where his camp was.

He thanked the Lord his fire was out, for they would have smelled the smoke for sure.

And they weren't Papagos. Reney thought he recognized one Papagos among them, Le-Cato, the new big chief or whatever they called him. But he couldn't be sure.

The Injuns rode on below him, the only sound their horses' huffing. Suddenly Reney felt the cold of the night, but again he thanked the Lord for that dead fire of his. . . .

He waited till the Injuns were well out of sight to the east, heading toward the mountains outside of Tucson.

Then, he rushed back to his camp, broke down his tent, and packed his horse.

If he was lucky, he could get back to the mining camp by morning. If Frawley didn't believe him, he'd go straight to the big man, Mates. Someone would take him seriously. The mining company would at least tell someone back in Tucson, and Fort Ranier would be alerted by telegraph, and the army boys would look into this thing, and do something about it. But that could take days.

Climbing up onto his horse, Reney wondered if that Negro Mullin knew about this, if this was why the man was here.

He shook his head. Don't think, get out. Get out and let the white men handle it.

"Wish I was back in Memphis."

Reining his horse around, Reney heard a sound above him, a scratch on the rocks.

Oh, Lord, they've found me.

But, looking up, he saw nothing.

Deciding not to wait and see, he urged the horse forward, out of the hollow, and turned it down the steep slope toward the plain below. Then he would ride a mile or so south, skirting the Injuns' path, then head at top speed toward the mining camp.

Again, something scratched above him on the rocks. A shape loomed up.

"What the — " Reney said, as a dark mass of feathers rose on the rock shelf above him, raised giant wings, then swooped down.

His curse was swallowed by the night, and even the Indian riders did not hear his single muffled scream as the thing covered and overwhelmed him.

Chapter Eighteen

Thomas awoke to the face of someone he didn't recognlze, a white woman with hair pulled back away from her face bending over him. She had kind blue eyes.

"Feel better?" she asked.

"Who — "

"Don't talk," the white woman said. She held a cloth in her hand, and she dabbed at his face with it. Thomas felt soothing coolness. The woman took the cloth away, dabbed it in a dish of water on a table next to the bed, and patted at him again. Only when Thomas tried to move any part of his face did he feel tightness and discomfort.

"I'm Mary, the Marshal's wife," the woman said, before he could speak again. "Your friend is in the other bedroom. Dr. Leonard set his broken leg. He's had a bit of a fever, but he'll be fine."

Thomas, feeling suddenly confined, tried to raise himself up on his elbow, but lay back with a groan.

The woman frowned, put her cloth down. "Don't do that again. You were beat up pretty

136

badly, Lieutenant. Is it all right if I call you that? Your friend Lincoln keeps calling you that in his delirium."

Thomas frowned, then nodded.

"I've got some soup on the kettle, I can get you some if you'd like."

Thomas nodded again. "Thank you," he tried to say, but the words came out garbled.

"Your lips are swollen," the woman said. She put the cloth down in the dish, turned, and left the room.

Thomas heard other noises. He was in a room which would normally be bright, with a large window next to the bed, now covered by a sheet. There was flowered wallpaper on the walls, shelves of knick-knacks, tiny potted cactus plants. A shelf of books lined the far wall.

A child's voice grew loud. Thomas turned toward the doorway to see a boy of four or five staring at him, eyes wide.

"The beat-up man is alive!" the boy exclaimed.

Thomas frowned at him. The boy turned and ran under the woman's arm as she returned, bearing a tray.

"Joshua, don't bother the Lieutenant!" she called after him. She added, "And your friends can't come in and look!"

"He's awake! He's alive!" the boy's retreating voice cried. Then Thomas heard the bang of a screen door.

"I'll try to keep him away from you," the woman said. She put the tray down on the table, started to spoon some of the soup out of a bowl so Thomas could eat it.

"I'll do that," Thomas said in a slur, having had enough of the nursing already, raising himself up on his elbows and staying there this time.

The woman hurriedly put the soup spoon down, reached out to help him. "I told you, you shouldn't — "

"Please," Thomas said, trying not to sound testy. He let the woman help him sit up, put a pillow behind his head.

The world momentarily spun, settled back into place.

"Lord . . ." Thomas muttered, hearing the word come out garbled.

"Your friend told me you were stubborn," the woman said disapprovingly.

Thomas found he could stay where he was without blacking out.

The woman lifted the tray, put it on his lap. When she tried to lift the soup spoon to his lips, Thomas reached out to take it from her.

"Please, I can — "

"All right!" the woman said. She put the

spoon down, threw up her hands. "If you need anything, call me," she said. "I'll be out front."

Trying to sound grateful, Thomas mumbled out, "Thank you. . . ."

The woman left the room, shaking her head.

On the second try, Thomas managed to get some of the soup to his mouth. His hands, his arms, didn't want to work. He felt as if his body had been rolled over by a heavy rock.

"Lord . . ."

The soup was good, though. Soon Thomas had regained some control over his limbs. He took a deep breath. His ribs hurt, too. Forsen had done a job on him, after all.

Outside the window, he heard children's whispering voices.

"He's in there, Nicky," one said. "He's right in there — and he's alive!"

"No way," another urgent whispering voice answered. "You made it all up, Joshua."

Wincing with the pain in his ribs, Thomas leaned over to the window and threw the shade up. He was met by two startled young faces.

He growled, making a face, then laughed as the two boys tore off away from the house.

"Can't be feeling too badly if you're up to scaring children," an amused voice said behind him.

He turned in bed to see Murphy in the doorway.

"Hello, Marshal," Thomas said.

Murphy said, "If it helps any, I've put a warrant out on Forsen. I've had him in here before. I'm sure when I get him again, he'll tell me who the other two with him were — that's the kind of man he is."

"Thank you."

"Don't thank me," Murphy said. "Because when you hear what I have to say next, you won't think so kindly of me. I'm afraid I'm going to have to ask you to leave off looking for Bill Adams's daughter. In fact, I'm going to have to ask you to stay here in Tucson till you feel better, then leave the area altogether."

Thomas gave Murphy a level look.

"I'm not real happy about it, but that's the way things are, Mr. Mullin. I've got my plate full with the President coming. I can't afford to have anything mar that. Call it a political thing, if you want."

"In other words," Thomas said, beginning to feel his mouth say the words the way they were supposed to sound, "you were ordered by Washington to get rid of me."

"Don't flatter yourself, Mr. Mullin," Murphy said. "The truth is, I was told by the President's advance men to make sure there was no trouble in the area with the Papagos.

140

They want a nice uneventful visit, something tidy and politically safe for the papers to talk about. And you've been stirring up too many hornets in the few days you've been here. Reeves told us about Bartow. We went out and got his body yesterday."

Thomas's mouth hurt but he talked anyway. "Did you know, Marshal, that someone at the Ranger Mining Company has been illegally selling arsenic to the Papagos? That's what produced the toxic effect we saw on Bill Adams's face. Bartow's, too."

Murphy got a pinched look. "I didn't know that."

"There's a lot more you don't know, Marshal."

"Such as?"

"Nothing I can say for sure, yet. What you have to do is give me more time."

Murphy sighed heavily. "I can't do that, Mr. Mullin. Like I said, when you're better, you'll have to leave." He wouldn't meet Thomas's eyes. "And I'm sorry, Mr. Mullin, I truly am."

Thomas rested the remainder of the day. Joshua and his young friend, Nicky, came back to mildly taunt him, and he played their game, growling at them whenever their faces rose above the windowsill outside. The one time he tried to rise on his own, he became dizzy and weak.

Mary Murphy came in at suppertime to feed him again. He hungrily ate what she offered. He could feel his body craving nourishment. After the meal, he fell back, exhausted, and slept.

During the night, he awoke, watching the moon rise. It was weakening, a thinning crescent.

Thomas lay back, letting bits of evidence wash over him. He had a lot of pieces, but they seemed to fit into different puzzles.

What would Holmes do?

Thomas knew what Holmes would do. He would conclude, logically, that there was only one puzzle, and one set of pieces. There were murders in the Boboquivari Mountains, specifically Kitt Peak. There was possibly Apache action. There was the illicit sale of arsenic to the Tohono O'otam. There was the mystery of Bill Adams, and his daughter. . . .

Wincing with the pain of movement, Thomas sat up, reached into his jacket at the end of the bed, and removed the letter from Bill Adams, opened it, and looked at it. He had previously dismissed it as having given up all its secrets.

She's all I have, Bill Adams had written, *and I don't want a terrible thing to happen.*

142

Thomas stared at the letter.

I don't want a terrible thing to happen.

Sherlock Holmes had said, "When you have eliminated the impossible, all that remains, however improbable, must be the truth."

Bill Adams had not said he didn't want a terrible thing to happen to his daughter.

He'd said, simply, he didn't want a terrible thing to *happen*.

"Damn," Thomas said, eliminating the impossible, and suddenly knowing where Adams's daughter was.

Thomas rose painfully and dressed. His clothes had been folded neatly on a chair at the end of the bed, along with this sidearm.

Bending to pull his boots on, Thomas nearly cried out at the pain but gritted his teeth and continued with the job. Then he stole out of the room, seeking the front door of the house.

On the couch in the parlor, the long form of Lincoln Reeves lay stretched out. His bandaged and splinted leg was propped over the far arm of the sofa. The young man snored loudly, and Thomas shook his head as he passed.

He eased open the front door and passed out into the night.

His horse was tied on the side of the house, still packed with provisions. His rifle was missing, though. Thomas checked his sixgun in the moonlight, rifled through his saddlebags until he found a box of cartridges, and moved it up where it would be in reach.

After two wincing attempts, he managed to climb up into the saddle and pull the reins around.

In an hour of slow riding, he had left Tucson behind, heading for the mountains.

Chapter Nineteen

The eagle waited for the white man.

Tomorrow night would be another night of sacrifice, as the moon dropped toward new. The eagle was ready for that. It knew that tomorrow night's would be the last sacrifice, because, soon, the eagle would have what it wanted. The Tohono O'otam would soon be strong and fly like the eagle, proud and brave. No one would call them Papagos — bean people — again.

And now, the white man came. He knew the path well, and sauntered up it singing, alone. The white man could not see in the darkness, by the light of the moon, like the eagle could, and so carried a lantern to guide him.

The eagle waited, prayed, looked at the sky.

Soon the white man had arrived, tying his donkey off on a stunted cottonwood, and coming the rest of the way alone. He carried the long box under his arm. The eagle fluttered its wings, looked at the box.

"So," the white man said, stopping a few feet away, below the rock shelf the eagle sat on. He put his lantern down and smiled, his face sickly yellow.

The eagle said nothing.

The white man shook his head and laughed. "You're really something, you know that? You want this, or not?"

The eagle nodded.

"Can't you speak? Hey, I'll tell you what. You say something, I'll let you have this for free. Deal?"

The eagle said nothing, and the white man threw back his head and laughed.

"Safe bet, heh?"

Again the eagle was silent, and the white man laughed.

"Well, time for business." The white man put down the box at his feet. He drew out a leather satchel tied to his waist, held it out. "Like I said, this is the last delivery you're going to get of this. That prying darkie somehow found out about it. Frawley at the mining camp don't want to mess with it anymore. He barely got out with this. From now on, whatever they have they keep for mining use, with strict records. Bastards don't want to go to jail."

The white man looked at the eagle, laughed.

"What's the matter, you sad?" He dropped the satchel on the ground, reached down, flipped open the lid on the box. "Don't be, look at this. It's what you wanted, right? Ordered it from New York myself. It's German. Best in the world."

The white man closed the box, slid it toward the eagle with the toe of his boot.

"Well? You got what I need?"

The eagle fluttered its wings, remained where it was.

The white man's face clouded.

"Hey, you don't pay, you don't buy."

He reached down to retrieve the box.

The eagle rose on its wings, dropped down upon the white man.

"Hey!" the white man shouted. The box fell to the side. The white man held his arms up to protect himself, then fell back. "What the hell you doing? You know who you're messing with?"

The white man fumbled his gun out of his holster as the eagle's claw came down across his hand, cutting it.

"Hey!"

The white man dropped the gun, looked up as the claw came slashing down again.

"You can't — !"

The eagle finished its work, pulled the white man's body to the edge of the cliff on its promontory, and pushed it over.

It watched the body plummet to the rocks below, then went back and retrieved the satchel and the box the white man had dropped.

The eagle went back to its promontory perch, fluttered its wings, looked at the sky.

"Soon," it said, and then dreamed as the night passed by.

Chapter Twenty

In Abilene, Texas, on the second leg of his trip west, President Theodore Roosevelt was ebullient. This was his country! God, how he loved it. The cowboys, the rodeo shows, the ranching exhibitions, it brought back nothing but good memories of a period in his life that had started bleakly and ended in the White House. This was a marvelous part of the United States! And if only Jenkins and Mawdrey would leave him alone and let him enjoy it! But there the two Secret Service men were, constantly hounding him, trying to keep him away from crowds, separating him from his people!

"I won't have it!" Teddy thundered again and again, and finally the two guard dogs would have to let him have his way. "This is a bully country, and I want to breathe it all in!"

Not to mention, gather those votes. For next year's election would be a doozy, and Roosevelt knew that the West might very well hold the key to the Republicans holding on to power.

"God, how I love it!" Roosevelt bellowed, turning to flash his smile at the crowd as he boarded the train west. The Texans were fine people, great people, and they had given him quite a show.

"Where to next?" Roosevelt said as the observation car's door closed behind him, leaving the crowd to look at bunting as the train pulled away. "Where in God's name do we go next?"

Roosevelt was like a little child, his eyes bright, unable to sit, bending to stare out the window and wave at the few who could see him.

"Tucson, Arizona, sir," Mawdrey said, in his slow drawl. While Roosevelt looked perpetually charged-up, Mawdrey looked perpetually half-asleep, except his eyes, which were always moving, always alert.

"Then up to Phoenix, over to California, then back through Wyoming," Jenkins finished. He was efficient, cool, and always awake, though seemingly without any enthusiasm at all, which drove Roosevelt to distraction.

"Wyoming! Bully!" Roosevelt cried. "And we're visiting my old ranch out there, right?"

Mawdrey looked to Jenkins, who checked down his list. "Exactly one week from now, sir. We've arranged for your old trail boss to be there, and some of the hands who worked at the ranch when you were there — "

"Absolutely bully!" Roosevelt shouted. He looked as though he were going to explode. "But next we go to — "

"Tucson, sir. Arizona."

"Wonderful country! Fine landscape. Saguaro cactus and piñon pine. Didn't we do something last year about the saguaro, protect it, or something?"

Jenkins said, "Yes, sir. You signed a law which will establish a national monument — "

"Can't wait to see it! Can't wait to see Tucson!" Roosevelt began to pace, as Mawdrey and Jenkins looked at each other and sighed.

"Who's for a game of gin rummy?" Roosevelt said, grinning, returning from the far end of the observation coach to hold a deck of cards under Mawdrey's nose.

"I suppose I am," the sleepy Secret Service man said, and Roosevelt looked over to Jenkins, smiling broadly, holding the cards out, until Jenkins threw up his hands and said, "Me, too, Mr. President."

Chapter Twenty-one

By morning, Thomas felt better. He had almost passed out twice during the night, once nearly tumbling from the saddle before pulling himself back up, wincing in pain, and taking a deep breath to focus his mind. But after finding and eating some of Bartow's jerky in his saddlebag, he had begun to feel some strength seep back into his limbs. Amazingly, after a second chew of the tough meat, he was nearly his old self.

He had once done a study of the various range foods, jerky included, and had decided that the chewy, stringy meat had, in its own small way, helped to settle the American West. More cowboys, settlers, and scouts had been kept alive with this nutritious, preserved food than any other; without it, many of them would have been forced to eat unknown native plants while on long rides, and probably taken sick. In lean times, when game was scarce, and in winter, when vegetables and edible plants were nonexistent, and especially in situations where provisions had to be light, and canned goods too bulky to pack, jerky had provided one of the only solutions. It was a remarkable, if saddle-like, food.

Thomas reached into his saddlebag, still cringing slightly at the pain in his limbs, and removed another chew. The sun was nearly up behind him. Ahead, the Baboquivari Mountains loomed closer, and one in particular, Kitt Peak, sat right in the middle of his path.

We have a date, my friend, Thomas thought.

In the purpling dawn, the approaching peak was balefully majestic. He could well see why the Tohono O'otam had come to consider it a sacred mountain. Though it barely towered over its neighboring crags, it dominated them in other ways. There was a brooding majesty to it, a solid perfection. Thomas had been in and around mountains for almost his entire Army career, but this peak commanded respect. Though he put little stock in what he basically considered superstition, he could understand why the Papagos had settled in the shadow of this monster, and considered it a holy place. He could understand why they feared it.

None of this, of course, prevented him from beginning the long climb to its peak.

The trails were well laid out. Yet, because of Kitt Peak's steepness, he made little progress in elevation. At midday he stopped to eat and rest, and found himself on a small promontory overlooking the Papagos reservation nestled at the base of the mountain below. He estimated he had climbed perhaps three thousand feet, though he might have covered five miles of trail.

The reservation looked deserted.

Thomas went to the edge of the promontory and studied the scene below. Not a sound was in the main street of the Papagos settlement; he could not make out a single figure or horse anywhere on the grounds. Wash was hung out to dry, but there were no cooking fires, nothing to indicate that anyone lived there.

Thomas scanned the area surrounding the reservation. Again, nothing. It was as if the entire tribe of the Tohono O'otam had disappeared.

Above and behind him, from the upper cliffs, Thomas heard a sound.

He turned and looked up.

A scatter of rocks had fallen from above, and was sliding down the face of the mountain. A wash of pebbles came to rest on his promontory, not far from where his horse stood tied.

Thomas slitted his eyes against the sun, sought to trace the path up to its sources.

The day, the mountain, were silent.

Thomas went back to his horse, finished a

chew of jerky, drank water from his canteen, and then proceeded.

The mountain rose under him, the day wore on.

Thomas began to hear flutterings above him, as if some bird were circling just above his head. But whenever he stopped to listen, the fluttering ceased. He studied the sky above the peak, but saw nothing.

He rode on.

Finally, as the sun was dropping toward the desert floor, the peak was in reach. The view below was majestic. Half of Arizona, it seemed, was spread out below him like a table setting, purple-hazed plains, and off to the north, some fifty miles off, the vague intimations of Tucson itself. Thomas stopped a moment to admire the view. None of the mountains in West Texas had quite approached this peak's height, or the magnificence of its 8,600-foot-high vista.

Above him, just over the lip of the peak, he heard the fluttering of wings, very close.

He turned as a winged thing dropped upon him, blotting out the sky. He was thrown from his horse, onto his back, and for a moment the pain of his beating screamed through his body, and he nearly blacked out. He felt something being forced into his mouth, and tried to spit it out, but his nostrils had been pinched, his mouth closed, and he swallowed the object.

He lay back as the winged thing rose off of him, and, momentarily, his strength began to return.

He rose up on his elbows, staring at the thing looking down at him; a painted figure wearing the feathered wings of a bird, a head-dress cowl of feathers, and a mask like a beak. Its leggings were covered with feathers, its feet sheathed in curving talons. Strapped to its side in a loop was a long curving blade like a sickle or claw.

Thomas made to get up. He found that suddenly his strength was leaving him again, his head growing light.

The feathered figure bent over him, slowly removed its cowled mask.

For a moment it stared at him with its black eyes.

"Thomas Mullin," it said finally, in clear, calm English. Thomas tried to work his now unworkable mouth, tried to get up. But everything failed him, and he felt himself laying back on what now seemed the featherbed of the rocky mountain floor, as the figure above him bent even closer, and said, in a not unkind, female voice, "My father told me so much about you."

Chapter Twenty-two

Lone Wolf was filled with pride. Before him, at the edge of the Papagos reservation, lay the naked wastes leading to Tucson. They had travelled unbothered, and now they stood on the verge of victory. Here, in the shadow of the mountain the white man called Kitt Peak, he could already feel triumph coursing through him. The great chiefs of old would be proud of him now; the great warriors would soon count him among their number. There was nothing now between himself and the city of Tucson, nothing that could stand in his way.

"Old man," he said, turning in his saddle to summon Le-Cato. Part of him told him to temper his pride, to show some deference for the chief of the Tohono O'otam, especially here in his own reservation; but part of him was too angry with the weakness he saw before him to be deferential.

Le-Cato, his face long, rode slowly up. Beside him was his granddaughter, the only member of the Tohono O'otam still in the reservation, who had ridden out to meet Le-Cato.

"Your people," Lone Wolf said, in mock

surprise, "why are they not here to greet us? Where," Lone Wolf said, letting his voice rise in anger, "is the great celebration I anticipated from the great and mighty Tohono O'otam?"

"My granddaughter has brought the things you wanted," Le-Cato said, indicating the bundles tied to his granddaughter's horse.

"Or is it," Lone Wolf continued in anger, "that your people are perhaps the Papagos, the bean people, after all?"

He raised his hand as if to strike the old man, who flinched away from his feigned blow and hung his head.

Lone Wolf laughed, turning back to the others. "Look around you!" he shouted. "Behold the majesty of the Tohono O'otam!"

There was laughter.

Lone Wolf turned his attention back to Le-Cato.

"Never mind, old man," he said, tempering his voice. "In your heart, I imagine you were a great chief to send your people away. In your heart, I suppose you saved your people. Since they are women and children, all of them, I suppose it was wise."

Suddenly his anger flared, and he did strike out, knocking the old man from his horse. There was more laughter as Le-Cato fell to the dust, his granddaughter jumping from her horse to help him up.

Lone Wolf jumped from his mount and pulled the trembling old man from his granddaughter's grasp. "Listen to me," he said, "and listen well."

Le-Cato looked away, until Lone Wolf grasped his chin, and pulled his eyes around to look into his own.

"There is one more thing for you to do, and then you can run off to hide with the other women and children. I will deal with your tribe later. But now, you will do the one thing we came here to do."

Le-Cato lowered his eyes.

"Do you understand me?" Lone Wolf shouted, pulling his blade from its sheath and holding it under the old man's throat. "Answer me with your mouth, or I'll cut your head off like a chicken's."

Le-Cato said, "Yes."

"Good." Lone Wolf let the old man go. He pointed up at Kitt Peak. "Now go into your sacred mountain, and meet your eagle." Suddenly he smiled, and motioned toward Le-Cato's granddaughter. "And, as a final offering to the eagle, take the squaw with you."

It was night-time when Le-Cato and his granddaughter reached the first plateau. The desert was already cold, and the old man shivered, as much with his mission as with the weather. Above him, the craggy mountain cut a line across the sky, slicing at the stars. Le-Cato shivered and walked on.

At the second plateau, an hour later, they heard a sound. Stopping, Le-Cato looked up fearfully, expecting the eagle to rise up above him and fall upon him. Silently he prayed that the eagle was not here, that it was flying high above the mountain and would not come down to him. For in what lay ahead he saw only disaster. Shivering, afraid, he climbed on.

Twenty minutes later, he paused. This time, he heard the sound he had feared, the rustling of feathers. Le-Cato was on the path leading to the next plateau. Tall above him, the mountain loomed like God himself.

"Eagle, are you there?" Le-Cato called out fearfully.

There was silence, and Le-Cato was about to walk on when a tall figure stepped out onto the path before him.

Le-Cato fell to his knees at the sight of the eagle. The wings fluttered high, and for a moment Le-Cato thought he saw the flash of a talon dropping toward him. Le-Cato saw darkness.

When he awoke, his granddaughter was gone, and there, at his foot, was a long wooden box.

"Is this the object I am to take to Lone Wolf?" Le-Cato shouted into the night.

Sadly, his heart sinking, he picked up the long box, turned, and made his slow way back down the mountain path.

Dawn had nearly come when the old man returned. Curling Smoke alone was awake, watching over the camp they had made. When he saw the old man stumbling toward him he ran to wake Lone Wolf, who lay sleeping in the shadow of his horse.

Lone Wolf hurried to meet the old man.

"So," he said, taking the long wooden box from Le-Cato's hands. "You have done something right, after all. Perhaps there is a spark of warrior left in your people yet."

Lone Wolf called to the others, who were now rising with the commotion.

"Come! Look at your future!"

Soon there was a gathering of braves around him. Lone Wolf fingered the wooden box lovingly before opening it. When he did pull the box's hinged lid back, he was overcome, and let out a whoop which was echoed by those around him.

He reached in gingerly to pull out the object within, cradling it in his arms.

"This," he said, "will change our nation of women into a nation of men."

Unable to control himself, he whooped again, holding the long, elegant, accurate stock of the Walthers repeating rifle with telescopic sight, the most accurate in the world, overhead.

"Go, my brothers," he shouted to the braves surrounding him. "Rise like the wind and bring word to all your tribes! Tell them to rise, and take their weapons with them! Before this day is done, the terrible blow will be struck!"

As the braves rode off to the four points, whooping wildly, leaving only a few behind, Lone Wolf turned to Le-Cato and said, "So, old man, let me tell you what I am going to do, and you can tell me now if you are truly my brother or not."

Chapter Twenty-three

Lincoln Reeves's leg told him not to move, but he didn't listen to it. At first, coming out of sleep, he thought he was at home, in his own bed, and that his leg had somehow fallen asleep. Then, beginning to come awake, he remembered where he was and thought he must be in the desert, and that a night of sleep on the hard ground had rendered his leg numb.

He tried to pull the leg back to him, and cried out in pain, coming fully awake, as his broken limb shifted in its cast.

"Lord, almighty — " a female voice said.

He remembered where he was now, and how he had gotten here — the fight, the painful ride back to Tucson, the painful setting of the leg, the fever . . .

A stern female face glared down at him.

"Sorry, Mrs. Murphy," Lincoln said meekly. "Guess I forgot my leg was broken for a moment."

"And that'll be the last time you forget!" Mrs. Murphy scolded. "I treasure your company, and your taking over my couch, but

I won't have you reinjuring yourself, just because you like my cooking so much!"

Lincoln smiled sheepishly.

"You heard what the doctor said — another day or two before you even move. Then another week of taking it easy after that." She pointed to the pair of crutches leaning against the couch. "You'll be up and using those before you know it."

"My wife — "

"Your wife was telegraphed yesterday." Mrs. Murphy fished into the front of her housedress, producing an envelope. "We got this last evening, after you were already asleep." She opened it, read: "Thank God the fool is not hurt more badly. I pray this will be the end of his adventures with that dangerous friend of his, Lieutenant Mullin. God bless you for your help. Please tell Lincoln his little boy misses him terribly."

Mrs. Murphy fixed Lincoln with a level stare. "I think someone else there misses you terribly, too."

"Yes, ma'am."

Mrs. Murphy handed him the telegram. "Now rest, and rest only."

As Mary Murphy was leaving the room, the Marshal entered, belting on his gun. He looked briefly at Lincoln, then at his wife.

"Mullin is gone."

"What?" Mrs. Murphy said.

"Must have rode out overnight. I swore the way he was beat up, he wouldn't be going anywhere for days."

"Don't be mad at yourself," his wife said.

Murphy's face was red. He said to Lincoln, "You think he was fool enough to ride up into that mountain alone?"

Lincoln hesitated, then said, "Yes."

"Glory be! What in damnation is wrong with that man?"

Lincoln said, "If you have the time, I'm sure my wife could tell you."

Murphy didn't laugh. "Well, I hate to say it, but he's on his own. I've got every man I can spare and more busy today with the President's visit." He looked hard at Lincoln. "I'm sorry."

"Don't worry too much about the Lieutenant," Lincoln said. "He knows how to handle himself."

Murphy snorted, and stomped away to the front door, opening it as one of his deputies was about to knock.

"Need you over at the office, Marshal. President's train is due in eight hours, and we're already swamped. Telegram from the Secret Service is there, they want things ready to go when Roosevelt gets in."

Murphy looked back at Lincoln briefly,

snorted again, and stomped out.

Mary Murphy had retreated to the kitchen; now she returned with a tray and with her son in tow. The tray she set down on the table in front of the couch.

"There's breakfast," she said, "and plenty of it, so eat. You told me yesterday how much you like my cooking. And, since I promised to take care of you, just so you don't get any foolish ideas about your friend, I've deputized little Joshua here to watch you."

The little boy glared hard at Lincoln. On his shirt had been pinned crookedly a small tin marshal's badge.

"He won't go nowhere, Ma," Joshua said.

"He won't go *anywhere,*" his mother corrected.

"Well, he won't," Joshua promised, continuing to glare.

The day wore on toward afternoon. Joshua kept his word, sitting on the edge of the couch, turning to stare hard at Lincoln every time he so much as twitched.

"Anyone tell you you look just like your dad?" Lincoln said.

"No talking," Joshua ordered.

After lunch, which they both ate off a tray, Mary Murphy got ready to go out. She came into the living room bearing a huge basket.

"I'm going over to your father's office," she said to Joshua. "Got to bring the men there something to eat. Then I've got a little marketing to do. Now I'm trusting you, Joshua. I'll be back in an hour at most."

Joshua saluted. "I'm on the job, Ma."

Mary looked at Lincoln, who pretended to sleep, then back at Joshua. "Good."

She went out.

"Got a checkerboard, Joshua?" Lincoln asked, sitting up. "Want to play checkers?"

"No talking," Joshua ordered.

Ten minutes later Joshua's friend, Nick, came by, banging through the front door, breathless.

"Josh, quick, come over t' my place! Willie's found a lizard, and he's getting it to change colors!"

Lincoln lay back, yawned, closed his eyes.

"Can't," Josh said.

"Are you *crazy?* It's a color changing lizard!"

"Got to watch the prisoner."

Lincoln feigned snoring.

"He's asleep!" Nick said. "My Mom said she'd watch you, if that's what you're worried about!" He studied Lincoln's prone form. "He'll be asleep for hours!"

"Well . . ."

"Come on!" Nick said, and ran out the door,

banging it behind him.

In a moment, Joshua had followed.

Lincoln opened his eyes. Carefully, wincing at the movement, he sat up on the couch. He reached over, took the crutches from their nesting place, put them under his arms, and tried to rise.

The first time he had to stifle a shout of pain as he put pressure on the broken leg, but the second time he had managed to stand, angling the leg back and putting pressure on the other leg.

He made his way to the door, opened it, and hobbled outside.

Cursing lightly, he stopped his progress, hobbled back into the house, searched the kitchen until he found a piece of paper and a pencil. He wrote a note to Mary Murphy, telling her where Joshua could be found, and left it on the couch. Again he hobbled to the door and went outside.

Around the side of the house was his horse. After what seemed an eternity, during which he was sure either Mrs. Murphy or Joshua would return, he managed to mount the saddle, tying the crutches down.

Keeping all pressure off the leg, he turned the horse and slowly headed out.

He was an hour out of Tucson, feeling weak

but proud of himself, when Marshal Murphy caught up with him. Red-faced, the marshal said nothing, but took the reins from Lincoln's hands, tied the horse to his own, and turned back around toward the city.

"Sorry for the trouble, Marshal," Lincoln said, and after a long while, Murphy said, "Don't be. I understand."

When they got back into town Murphy passed his own house, pausing as Mary Murphy and Josh came out. Mrs. Murphy said resignedly, "Thank you for the note, Trooper," while Joshua hung his head in shame. They rode on to the Marshal's office, where a deputy came out to help Lincoln down off his horse.

"Put him in the first holding cell," Murphy said, and the deputy answered, "Yes, sir."

"Lock it, and make sure it's locked."

The deputy nodded.

"Bring me the key."

"Yes, sir."

"And put his crutches where he can't find them."

"Yes, sir," the deputy said again.

"Marshal — " Lincoln said.

"Don't say anything. Just go."

Looking chagrined, trying to keep his weight off the leg, Lincoln went into the jail.

Chapter Twenty-four

Vaguely, as if from far away, Thomas felt someone putting something into his mouth. He felt his head being lifted, then felt the coolness of water running around his lips.

"Drink," someone, very far away, said. "Swallow."

He moved his lips, felt water run into his throat, and something hard riding it down into his gullet.

"Good."

His head was laid back down.

He opened his eyes, but they wouldn't work on their own. They seemed to swivel this way and that, and when he tried to focus them, they slid off independently. Finally, he gave up trying to control them, and they reached a kind of stasis on their own. Suddenly they did focus, directly overhead, and he saw burning bright pinpoints of light, stars that seemed to burn through the night.

"You're going to dream, Lieutenant Mullin," the faraway voice said. "You're going to dream like my people have dreamed for a thousand years."

The voice was soothing, not menacing at all.

Again he felt his head lifted, felt something cradled beneath his neck. His bedroll? He was flat on the ground now, his head supported so that he could see in front of him.

Sherlock Holmes.

That was it. He felt like Sherlock Holmes, after the famous detective had taken cocaine. Was this what cocaine felt like? He didn't know. Somewhere deep in the back of his mind, though, he knew that he must stay alert, must analyze. Was that why Sherlock Homes took cocaine, to analyze?

No, it was because of ennui, because his mind was not being challenged.

Was Thomas's mind being challenged?

Yes, it was. He had come up here to solve a mystery.

"Adams . . ." he said, his own voice sounding very far away, as at the far end of a tunnel.

"Don't speak. Listen. Watch."

Suddenly his mind went flat. "Yes . . ."

In front of him, on the crested plain of Kitt Peak, he saw the feathered figure of a human being, outlined by night, rocks, and stars. The figure began to dance, and sing.

"Many suns ago, our forefathers soared like the birds," the figure said, and suddenly Thomas was transported, through the singing and dancing, to another world. He saw a proud people on a desert plain, dancing under the sun in the wide shadow of a sacred mountain; they wore feathered head-dresses and on their hands and feet were the claws of eagles. And these dancers now rose up off the ground, spreading their wings wide, and flew up into the very air, and began to soar. They became one with the clouds, making rings around the sacred mountain, and then up to the sun —

The figure before Thomas danced and sang, and Thomas saw the proud people, the Tohono O'otam, fall back to earth. Some of them died, and others were stripped of their wings and talons as they stuck the earth. They were left naked, and ran from the sun, hiding in the cracks and caves of the mountains, sneaking out to plant beans before the sun rose high —

The winged figure danced before Thomas, the song becoming choked with sadness. Other tribes swooped down upon the Tohono O'otam, and ravaged them, and stole their goods. Then a blue-suited swarm of white men came, and herded them like cattle, pushing them up against the sacred mountain until they were pressed tight into its cracks and fissures. And soon, very soon, they began to grow old and die. . . .

"I hated my father for what he was," the voice said, becoming suddenly very close and loud. Thomas saw the beaked mask of the eagle close by his own face. "Growing up, I lived with the people the white men called the *Papagos,* the bean people, and I saw what it had done to them. What it had done to my mother. I saw both worlds, and I liked the world of the Tohono O'otam better, even though the other squaws called me half-breed.

"It was a world of dreams, of the past, but these were people of God. They came from the earth, and the sky, and they were destroyed when their dream world was destroyed. I wanted to bring that dream world back to them."

The masked face was very close. In Thomas's mind, it filled the whole of the earth, stretching from horizon to horizon, from earth to the stars.

"Do you understand what I'm saying, Lieutenant Mullin? I think you do. I hated my father, yet I loved him. He spoke very highly of you, and I think you know what I'm talking about. The Tohono O'otam will be a great tribe again. They will fly with the eagles again. I think you know what it's like to be an outsider, to want to soar, but be tied to the earth by the white man. The white man doesn't matter, the Apache doesn't matter. After what happens tomorrow, the foolish Apache will be hunted from the earth. The white men will never let Lone Wolf get away with what he will do. In Lone Wolf's mind he is a great chief, but he is only foolish. When he is gone, this land will be free for my people again, and we will return to the land of dreams."

"You're . . . mad," Thomas heard himself saying, from a great distance away. "You killed those young women out of revenge for how they treated you when you were young. The arsenic has made you . . . mad."

"You're wrong," the masked face said. "The arsenic has made me powerful. It made me see who I am. Do you know where I read about it? In the white man's school. I found it in a book. The Arsenic Eaters in the mountains of Austria have taken it for centuries, and it has made *them* strong."

"You're . . . insane. . . ."

The huge masked face pulled back a little. Again Thomas felt his mouth being opened, something forced in, followed by the wetness of water from his canteen. The masked face pulled all the way back.

"Dream your own dreams, Thomas Mullin," the eagle said. "I have given you only peyote. I will return with something for you to see, before you must die."

The eagle raised its wings; Thomas closed

his eyes, and when he opened them the eagle was gone.

And Thomas dreamed. He saw many things in his dream. In it, he was Sherlock Holmes, in deerstalker cap, pacing through a room that looked like both his aunt's house in Boston and 221B Baker Street. A pile of magazines lay on a table; when he approached, he saw that they were *Strand* magazines, with his own face on the cover, holding a magnifying glass. A banner across the top of the magazine read, "New Thomas Mullin mystery inside!" On the mantle of the fireplace was a Persian slipper holding tobacco; he filled his calabash pipe and lit it. His violin lay cradled on his favorite chair. He picked it up, put it under his chin, and began to play. . . .

For a long time, he listened to the music. Characters appeared before him, dancing. Bill Adams was there, dancing with his Indian scout friend, Tahini. Both of them had horrible rictal grins frozen on their faces. Lincoln Reeves appeared, in his cast, dancing awkwardly with Mary Murphy. Marshal Murphy looked on, scowling under his red locks. The little Murphy boy, Joshua, wove between the other dancers. All of them were turning toward him; he thought they were urging him to play faster, so he did. They continued to speak, but he could not hear them above the music. In the dream, he closed his eyes for a moment, and saw a whirling emptiness within himself. Suddenly he knew why Holmes took cocaine. He saw the same emptiness of inaction within himself. He saw the same fear of inactivity, the same ennui that came when he was not challenged. It was a hole that had to be filled with something. Suddenly, he knew himself better than he ever had. And he knew what the crawling, tingling feelings of superstition he had felt were. They were not fear of the unknown. Bill Adams's daughter did not know of the unknown any more than he did. No one did. The unknown was beyond the pale. Holmes would not deal with it, because it was irrelevant to him. It either was there or it was not, but to Holmes it did not interfere in the everyday, which was where Holmes had to operate. For Thomas it was the same. It was not the unknown that had scared him; it was himself. And now he saw himself better than he ever had; knew that, like Holmes, it was inactivity, the lack of challenge, that would destroy him. . . .

He heard voices calling to him above the music. He opened his eyes, and saw the dancing spinning fast before him as he played a kind of devil's trill on the violin. And yet the dancers were trying to call to him as they spun, trying to tell him something, trying to make all the puzzle pieces fit —

"The President."

Suddenly Thomas stopped playing, and knew what was happening. It was his own mouth that had told him the answer. The Apaches, an Apache chief named Lone Wolf, was going to kill President Roosevelt when he visited Tucson tomorrow. The dancers began to disappear before him, fading into dreams, Bill Adams last, waving a sad good-bye, mouthing words to Thomas as he faded. "I wanted you to come out here to help me hunt down my daughter, Thomas. She always took peyote and had strange dreams. But it was the arsenic that changed her. She started with a little, and then more and more. It made her believe she could act out her dreams. Cates got the arsenic from Frawley. Abby paid them. All of the money the Tohono O'otam made went to Cates, and Abby also supplied Cates with peyote, which he sold to other tribes. That was Forsen's job. I found out, Thomas, I found out and my own daughter killed me. She killed Tahini, and Bartow too. . . ." until Bill, too was gone, and then the room faded, 221B Baker Street dissolving into mist, leaving rocks and starry sky, but still the voice of someone calling, someone shouting in the real world. . . .

The eagle reappeared, dragging another figure, a young girl, with it. The girl thrashed in the eagle's grip, screaming, trying to break free, and the eagle threw the girl to the ground, slashing across her leg with the talon-like blade it held. The girl cried out, fell to the ground, gripping her leg.

The eagle approached Thomas, who now felt the dreams fading. He saw hard rocks and the stars fading in a dawning sky. Yet when the eagle came close, he feigned drunkenness, looked into the eagle's eyes as if the drug was still upon him.

"Good," Bill Adams's daughter said. "You have dreamed, and are dreaming." She reached into her costume. "In a little while, I must give you the final dream, with this." She held a peyote bud coated with gray powder. "But first I will show you how greatness is returning to my people, how I have made them great again by letting them worship me."

She raised her wings, turned back to the young girl who lay panting on the ground, looking up at the eagle in terror.

The eagle dragged the protesting girl to the edge of the promontory and lay her there. She turned around to face Thomas, outlined by the growing dawn.

"Behold the greatness of the eagle!" she cried, drawing out two long talon blades and holding them high in her out stretched wings. The girl below her shrieked as the eagle brought the blades down.

Thomas drove himself forward at the eagle, striking it as the blades came down, missing the girl. The eagle did not go down. Thomas grabbed at the winged hands and the two blades were dropped to the ground. Thomas fell back, lay on the ground as the eagle rose and turned on him. At his feet were the two blades, and he picked them up. He stood, crouching, waiting for the rush.

"So dreams have not been enough for you," Bill Adams's daughter said sadly. "From the way my father spoke of you, I thought you would understand me."

Breathing hard, the blades in front of him, Thomas waited.

"I'm going to have to bring you in to Tucson," he said.

"Of course." She reached into her costume, produced the peyote bud laced with arsenic, and put it in her mouth. Then she raised her wings up high, turned, and leapt from the promontory, shouting, "I fly for my people, into the sun!"

Thomas rushed to the edge of the promontory and looked down. For a moment, his mind thought it saw the winged body arch out into soaring flight toward the rising sun, as it shouted in exultation. Then there was a short scream, and what had only been illusion became reality, as the body was dashed on the rocks below, and lay finally silent; a white, crushed figure in the morning of the new day.

Thomas turned, panting, to look at the terrified young girl who lay holding her leg, looking up at him.

"Is it over?" the girl asked, fearfully.

Thomas dropped the talon-blades. In his mind, the drug still swirled, leaving him weak and disoriented. For a moment he thought he was back in 221B Baker Street, and had to shake his head to clear it.

"No, it's not," he said to the young girl, as he helped her to her feet. "It's just begun."

Chapter Twenty-five

Lone Wolf was in position by three o'clock. It had all gone flawlessly. Two miles outside of Tucson, they had changed into the clothes from the mining camp, and, when they were finished, they looked like any other Indian scouts working for the company who had come into Tucson for the day. The spot that had been selected was perfect; hidden and unobtrusive, and far enough away so that no one would even check it. That was the beauty of the Walthers rifle; an accurate shot at three hundred yards was not only possible but expected. Through the sight, the platform next to the train station laid out in bunting was square between the crosshairs. And on the top floor of this hotel, the farthest from the train station in the city, a hotel that was often used by Indian scouts because of its unsavory location and cheapness, no one would give them a second thought.

"Le-Cato was an old fool, but he did well in reserving our place here," Lone Wolf said, thinking of the old man he had left lying in the sun. Perhaps after all of this, he would go back and give the old fool a chief's burial. He had died like a dog, but perhaps he deserved to enter the afterlife with dignity.

Perhaps.

Lone Wolf leaned out of the open window and glanced down at Curling Smoke, who stood out on the street, watching to see if any interference would come. The old brave nodded up at Lone Wolf, signaling that all was well. So, too, did the others who lounged against poles or sat feigning sleep under eaves up the street, halfway to the train station.

All was well. All would be well.

Lone Wolf felt an excitement course through him. This was like a buffalo hunt. He had heard somewhere that this President, Theodore Roosevelt, had hunted buffalo, and had spent time in the West. Perhaps, then, he would know what it was like to be the buffalo as he died, how the hunted felt.

Looking through the Walthers sight again, zeroing in on the bunting-festooned platform, Lone Wolf had to suppress a warrior's shout. When the fat little white man, the buffalo, stepped out onto that platform —

"Soon," Lone Wolf hissed, between his teeth, hearing the assents from his braves behind him. "Very soon."

Chapter Twenty-six

"Bully!"

Mawdrey winced. It was hard enough for the Secret Service man to take care of the President when he was merely doing his job. It was much worse when Roosevelt became enthusiastic, which was most of the time. But it had been even worse lately, since this western trip had brought out something in Roosevelt even beyond enthusiasm. Mawdrey himself couldn't understand it — every town and city they'd been to looked much same: dry, drier, and driest — but the President had worked himself into a veritable rapture, and seemed to be soaking up every drop of whatever there was in this Godforsaken country to drain — certainly not water.

And now . . . Tucson. The city, flat and wide, nestled into the bowl of a nearby arid mountain, was growing slowly in view ahead. Already Roosevelt had been hanging half out the window of the observation deck, studying the tired-looking saguaro cactus, waving at a startled rancher, who had stopped to study the presidential train as it chugged by.

"Mr. President," Mawdrey attempted.

"I said absolutely *bully!*" Roosevelt shouted, as he moved from window to window, staring out at the scenery. "Look at that sky! Look at that desert floor, those mountains! My *God,* it's all magnificent!" He pointed in the distance. "What is that huge peak, there? Isn't it a marvel? Jenkins, find out what it is!"

Jenkins rolled his eyes, walked to the window, looked out, went back to study a geological map rolled out on a table.

"It's . . . Kitt Peak, I believe, sir — "

"Marvelous! Solid as granite!"

"There's some talk about erecting an astronomical observatory there, perhaps the National Observatory itself. But there's been some trouble with the local Indians — "

"Trouble? What trouble?"

"It's considered a sacred peak by the Papagos, who have their reservation nearby — "

"Trouble?" Roosevelt shouted. "There can't *be* trouble! I won't *allow* trouble! Put it on your list! Let's get it fixed, make everybody happy! Is that — "

Roosevelt was peering intently out of one of the windows, looking down toward the desert floor near the tracks. Suddenly, he threw the window open, leaned halfway out, opening Mawdrey's sleepy eyes wide, sending the Se-

184

cret Service man leaping forward to hold Roosevelt from climbing straight out of the window.

"Mr. President — !"

"A roadrunner! By God, I saw a roadrunner! Capital!"

Roosevelt pulled himself back into the railroad car, moved to a window on the opposite side of the train, peered out.

"What time do we get in?" he asked Jenkins, who checked his watch, and then a timetable laid out next to the map.

"Forty minutes from now," Jenkins said. "Exactly four o'clock. The University of Arizona has a new band, and they will play a short tune while you step off the train. Then you will speak for four minutes."

"Bully! Isn't that saguaro magnificent!" Roosevelt shouted. He had already moved to another window, and stood with his nose pressed against it, the desert sun glinting off his spectacles.

Jenkins rolled his eyes.

Chapter Twenty-seven

Even with Thomas's horse, it took them three hours to climb down from Kitt Peak.

The Tohono O'otam squaw's name was Morning Rain. At first she was in shock, but after Thomas bandaged her leg she became merely uncommunicative. Thomas could get nothing from her, though he tried to get across to her the severity of her position.

"We're talking about the President of the United States," he said. "If this attempt to kill him succeeds, don't you realize what this will mean for your people? This won't free them — it will enslave them. They'll be hunted, along with everyone else who was involved. The United States Army will never quit until every member of your tribe is in chains. This will wipe out your people, even though they weren't responsible."

Morning Rain stared straight ahead, either uncomprehending or unwilling to tell Thomas what he needed to know.

But when they reached the bottom of the trail at the base of Kitt Peak, and found the body of Le-Cato lying in the sun, her reactions changed.

"Grandfather!" she shouted, jumping from the horse. She went to the old man's body and lifted the unseeing head. She began to cry, then cradled the old chief's head to her breast, rocking back and forth, singing softly.

Thomas watched her, then said, "I have to go."

She said nothing, until he turned his horse to ride off.

"I will tell you," she said suddenly. "I will tell you what you need to know, then I will bring my people back to the reservation, and bury my grandfather. I heard what they said. I heard everything."

Thomas listened, as she told him.

Chapter Twenty-eight

When the band began to warm up down the block, Marshal Murphy came to see Lincoln in his cell. Peering through the bars, he said, "Think I can trust you?"

Lincoln grinned sheepishly.

Murphy said, "President Roosevelt's coming in twenty minutes, and I'd hate for you to miss it. Thing is, you have to promise me you won't try to ride off, or do anything foolish."

"I'd like to see that, Marshal. I promise."

"I'm taking you at your word, Reeves. If you break your promise to me, I guarantee you, you'll be back in this cell for real, on charges."

Mary Murphy and little Joshua appeared in the doorway, and Murphy turned to his son. "This is your chance to redeem yourself, son. I'm putting you in charge of the prisoner, and this time I don't want you to let him out of your sight."

Joshua looked up from the floor. "Yes, sir."

"Good."

Murphy motioned to one of his deputies,

who produced the crutches and unlocked the cell.

"Remember what I said," Murphy said to Lincoln as he hobbled past. "This time I mean it."

"Yes, sir," Lincoln said, saluting the Marshal.

Outside, it was like a circus day. The whole city had turned out, and was filling the street in front of the train station, below a podium draped in flags. In front of the podium, the band continued to tune up, playing "Dixie" to a mingling of laughter, hissing, and scattered cheers.

"Mr. Roosevelt is a great man," Mary Murphy said as they walked.

Lincoln looked down at little Josh, who was scowling at him intently.

"I think your son has learned his lesson, ma'am," Lincoln said to Mary Murphy.

"Oh, yes," she answered. "He never makes the same mistake twice, right, Joshua?"

"I got a whoopin' 'cause of you," Josh said to Lincoln, still scowling. He held up a six-gun carved from a piece of wood. "This time I shoot to kill."

But sure enough, on their way up the street, Josh met his friend, Nick, who begged him to come with him.

"We've got a space right up front, where the President's gonna talk!" he said.

Joshua looked up at his mother, pleading.

"It's the best spot in the whole place!" Nick went on. "You'll be able to see the President spit!"

"Aw, Mom . . ." Josh said.

His mother threw up her arms. "All right, Joshua, you can go."

"Great!" He pressed his six-gun into his mother's hand and ran off with his friend.

"Looks like I guard you alone," Mary Murphy said to Lincoln, holding up the gun. "And I warn you, Mr. Reeves, *I* shoot to kill, also."

"Yes, ma'am."

Already, they could hear the distant whistle of the train. Lincoln followed the line of the tracks and there, just crawling into view at the edge of the city, was the President's festooned train, the brightly colored Southern Pacific engine pulling three dark-green coaches. People lining the tracks began to cheer, and, briefly, a figure appeared, leaning from one of the windows in the last car, waving.

"He sure does know how to put on a show," Lincoln said.

Ten minutes later, the streets now swelling with people, the band began to play, a ragged tune that quickly resolved itself into

"Hail to the Chief."

In the hotel up the street, Lone Wolf pressed his eye to the Walthers's sight. Ragged strains of music reached him. Below, on the street, his warriors had signalled that the train had stopped. It would not be long. Squinting through the gunsight, Lone Wolf could see the rear platform of the observation car, the door opening slightly, then closing again as a bland, thin man in a suit stepped out. It was not the President, and Lone Wolf's finger eased slightly on the trigger. He was pleased that he had a clear shot to the train. If he chose, he could shoot the President even before he reached the podium and gave his silly speech. But that would not be dramatic. He would wait until the little man was at the height of his glory, giving the white crowd what they had come to see, smiling under his mustache, holding his hands out over the cheering masses. Then Lone Wolf would cut him down, not as a buffalo after all, but a dog.

Lone Wolf smiled to himself, and kept the Walthers steady on the sill of the window.

The crowd pressed forward. Lincoln and Mary Murphy were about halfway up, with a good view, about as good as they thought it would get. But suddenly, a pushing figure appeared in the crowd, Josh and his friend, Nick. They stopped breathless in front of Mary and Lincoln.

"Mom! Mom! The President wants to meet me! And him, too!" Josh said, pointing excitedly at Lincoln.

"What?" Mary Murphy said.

"It's true!" Josh shouted, and his friend, Nick, said, "Yes, it's true!"

Mary looked over the crowd toward the podium, and saw her husband gesturing at her. Beside him was a thin man in a suit, holding a pad of paper.

"Well . . ." Mary Murphy said.

"Come on, Mom! Come on!" Josh said, tugging at her.

They made their way through the crowd, Lincoln cutting a wide swath with his crutches while Mary apologized for making people move. Soon they had reached the front of the podium, and Marshal Murphy was reaching down to help them up onto the stage.

"Roosevelt wants to hold Josh while he's speaking, and introduce Lincoln as a hero of the Indian wars and Abraham Lincoln's namesake," the Marshal said.

"Well, all right," Mary Murphy said, a bit overcome. Josh was helped up onto the podium, then disappeared, running, into the door of the observation car, while Lincoln was assisted onto the podium.

"Just stand there and look heroic," the thin man in the suit, who then introduced himself as Jenkins, said.

Another man, taller, with a sleepy-looking face but hard eyes, emerged from the observation car and closed the door behind him. From the car emerged a loud bellow, the word, "Bully!"

The tall man leaned over to Jenkins and said, "He'll be out in a minute. He's showing the boy his Indian arrowhead collection."

"Lord," Jenkins said, then he made a motion at the bandleader, who immediately started his people into "Hail to the Chief" again.

The door to the train's observation car opened wide.

There was nothing for a moment.

Then, to wild applause, Roosevelt emerged, smiling widely, striding to the podium with little Josh on his shoulders.

Lone Wolf pressed his eye painfully to the Walthers gunsight. There was much movement on the platform at the back of the train, white men and one black man moving into his view. Then, suddenly, the white man's President appeared, with a child on his shoulders.

To Lone Wolf, it made no difference. His finger poised hard on the trigger, and he moved the rifle smoothly to follow them the few steps to the podium, and stop there, the crosshairs centered on the President's head, and the white child's belly behind it.

The band, at a motion from Jenkins, ceased playing. "American friends!" Roosevelt boomed. "In this great wide country, in this, the greatest of countries, I am *proud* to be with you today!"

The band played a few bars, and the crowd cheered wildly. Roosevelt laughed, looking up at Josh as the boy clapped, balancing himself on the President's shoulders.

Roosevelt waited for the cheers to subside. "Proud, and *happy* as all getdown! And though my home is that big white one in the East, I want to tell you that my heart will *always* be in the West! Because here is where America really made itself. The East, if you think about it, was created by Englishmen and Spaniards. But the West was created by Americans!"

Again the band played a few notes, to wild cheering. Roosevelt, laughing like a child, bounced Josh up and down on his shoulders.

Suddenly the President reached out sideways and pulled Lincoln, who stood a little dazed by what was happening, toward him. Lincoln almost got caught up in his crutches, but moved to stand next to Roosevelt. He felt a strong, thick arm encircle his waist, hold him tight as a cobra.

"How are ya!" Roosevelt whispered, but before Lincoln could answer, the President was already addressing the crowd again, his voice booming out over the street.

"Yes, America is the greatest country God ever put on this earth! And I'd like to introduce to you one of the men who helped create the West, who forged his way through the dangers and hardships, so that wonderful people like you could live and prosper here!"

More blaring music from the band, more cheering. Lincoln found himself smiling, and holding up his hand to wave, as Roosevelt's rock hard grip, behind his back, was urging him to do.

With a sinking feeling Thomas Mullin heard the strains of band music waft over the desert to him. He was still a mile out of Tucson, and feared he was too late. The only chance he had was the fact that Roosevelt might talk for a while. From what Morning Rain had told him, Lone Wolf would seek the dramatic in his act.

Every step of the horse sent pain through

Thomas, which he ignored. The ride back toward Tucson had been one of the hardest, fastest, of his life. And the effects of the drug Bill Adams's daughter had given him had not completely worn off. He found himself constantly shaking his head to clear it, his mind wandering off toward dreams. At times he thought the earth was opening up before him, ready to swallow his horse; twice he pulled back on the reins, sure he was at the edge of a precipice. But still he rode on.

When he heard the band stop playing, then heard a cheer from a distant crowd, he shook his head vigorously, spurred his horse on, and, ignoring the pain that shot through him, rode faster.

"Friends!" Roosevelt shouted, gripping Lincoln by the shoulder. "This man is a hero, and all of *you* are heroes, too! For together you have forged the greatest nation on earth! And before I leave you today, I want to pledge to you that all of us, *together,* will continue to build this nation, and add even more greatness, more strength, more courage, to what we already have! The world envies America — and rightly so — God bless you all!"

Lone Wolf's finger drew tightly on the Walthers's trigger. The crowd in front of the train station was cheering wildly, beginning to surge forward. The American President was holding the black man closely with one hand, waving high overhead with his other, smiling broadly. The white child on his shoulders waved, too. This was the moment Lone Wolf had waited for, the President in his glory, his head above his smiling foolish mouth centered in the crosshairs as Lone Wolf pulled his finger back on the trigger —

There was only time for Thomas to react. He tore into the edge of Tucson, spotting the hotel Morning Rain had told him about. Circled around it in the street, trying to look casual, were four Apaches. There was no time to think. The crowd in the near distance was cheering wildly, the band playing loud.

Thomas rode hard into the middle of the street in front of the hotel, jumped from his horse. A momentary shock greeted him — it seemed the ground below him had opened up again, showing a depth of blue sky and clouds, an eagle circling below him. He shook his head as he struck the dust. Time seemed to slow. He drew his gun from its holster, rolled, looked up at the windows on the top floor of the hotel, locating the one that was open. The long slim barrel of a rifle protruded from it. He saw the crouching figure of Lone Wolf behind its gunsight. In his drugged state, Thomas imagined he could hear the rifle go off. But it was his own gun firing, and a moment later he saw a puff of smoke from the rifle barrel.

Then the world exploded around him. He saw one of the Apaches running toward him, knife out; saw another coming from the opposite direction. There was pandemonium behind him. The noises got very loud. His eyes began to cloud. The final vision he had was of an old Apache leaping toward him, long knife in hand —

"Down!" Mawdrey shouted. For a moment Roosevelt thought he was shot, and thought immediately of the young boy on his shoulders. He felt himself pushed to the floor of the platform, felt warm blood on his face.

"The boy!" he shouted. But Mawdrey was already covering him. Roosevelt put his hand to his face and drew it away. It was covered in blood. But when he looked up he saw the black man, Lincoln, still standing, dazed, holding his crutches, a spread of blood rising through his shirt at the shoulder.

"Attend to that man!" Roosevelt shouted, thrusting Mawdrey off him, turning to see the boy's mother holding the lad, pulling him close to her.

"He's all right," the woman said. "He's all right."

Roosevelt stood, caught Lincoln as he collapsed, his crutches sliding away from him.

"Sorry, Mr. President . . ." Lincoln said.

"Nonsense!" Roosevelt shouted. "My God, a hero again!"

Lincoln nodded weakly, and then fell to unconsciousness.

Chapter Twenty-nine

Thomas awoke, after what seemed a very long sleep, in the same bed in Marshal Murphy's house he'd had before. For a moment he thought he had never left, and that everything that came rushing back at him that had happened on Kitt Peak and in Tucson had been merely a dream. But when he tried to sit up, and felt the bolt of hot pain shoot through the bandaged wound in his right shoulder, he knew he had not been dreaming.

Mary Murphy appeared with her habitual tray of food.

"You should be hungry, Lieutenant," she said, matter-of-factly. "You've been asleep for two days."

"Two days!"

He slid back down in the bed, finding a spot to accommodate his sore shoulder and aching head.

"That's right," Marshal Murphy said. "Your friend, Lincoln, only slept twenty-four hours. Doctor Hazeltine said you were under the influence of some drug, and might not come awake for days."

"Lincoln — "

"He's fine," Marshal Murphy said. "Wounded in the shoulder, like you. The bullet missed Roosevelt by eight inches. You killed Lone Wolf, you know. You also saved the President's life and my son's, who was on Roosevelt's shoulders at the time."

Thomas grunted.

"Don't you want to know what happened to you?"

"I take it the Apache who attacked me was not accurate with his knife thrust."

"My God, man, you fought him off! There were two Secret Service men a half block away, along with one of my men, but they didn't get there until it was nearly over. Two of the Apaches were captured, the other two killed. You were raving about falling through the sky, an eagle — "

"The peyote," Thomas said. "It was unpleasant, and powerful."

"I take it you have some story to tell me, when you're up to it," Marshal Murphy went on. "We went up to the Papagos reservation yesterday, found a couple of bodies at the base of Kitt Peak. One of them was Cates, the other Bill Adams's daughter."

Thomas said, "Le-Cato, the Tohono O'otam chief, was killed, also. He was something of a hero, in the end."

"He was being buried when we got to the reservation. When you're up to it — "

"Yes, we'll talk later, Marshal."

"Good."

Josh appeared, bearing a book. He went to Thomas, and laid it on the bed, then ran out.

"A present," Marshal Murphy said, "from the President. He wanted badly to meet you, but had to move on. Had a campaign schedule to meet. They're trying to downplay the incident. In fact, they control the press, and they're going to make believe it didn't happen. There's an election coming up, and they don't want anything to mar Roosevelt's western trip. But the President wanted you to have that."

Grunting with the pain it caused him, Thomas turned the book over. It was a leather-bound edition of *The Adventures of Sherlock Holmes*. Inside the flyleaf was written, "To a bully fellow, a real man, from one Holmes admirer to another." It was signed, "Theodore Roosevelt."

"It was his own copy, which he'd brought along on the trip," Marshal Murphy said. "You'll also be happy to learn we captured your friend, Forsen, and his buddies. Frawley's in custody, too, though we're pretty sure he knew nothing about the plot against

Roosevelt. I can guarantee he'll spend time in jail, though. There are Army contingents already rounding up the rest of Lone Wolf's braves."

Thomas nodded, put the book aside. "I must thank the President. . . ."

His eyes were heavy, and when he forced them open a few moments later, before falling back to sleep, Marshal Murphy and his wife were leaving the room.

Later, he awoke, and felt wide awake. The sun was still up, and he heard sounds outside the house. Moving slowly from the bed, he saw outside the curtains the marshal in the back, chopping wood, little Joshua running around as his mother hung wash.

With slow steps, Thomas made his way to the front room. The shades were drawn, but Lincoln was in the spot Thomas had left him in the last time, leg in a cast up on the end of the sofa. A new bandage covered his right shoulder. He turned and grinned at Thomas as he entered the room.

"Hello, Lieutenant."

"Seems we can form a shoulder wound club, Trooper."

"Yes, sir."

"You feeling fit?"

"Will in a week or so. Mrs. Murphy was

kind enough to wire Matty. I'm afraid she made me sound like a hero for taking a bullet I didn't know was coming. Matty's heading out here herself to fetch me back home." He grinned. "I don't think she trusts you at all, Lieutenant."

"I don't blame her, Trooper."

"What are you going to do now, Lieutenant? When it's time to move on, I mean?"

Thomas frowned. "I don't quite know. but I think I'll be staying out in this part of the country. There's too much of it in me, I'm afraid."

Lincoln sighed. "I know what you mean, sir."

Thomas raised his eyebrows. "Don't tell me you're thinking of giving up sharecropping?"

"I'll have to talk it over with Matty, first, but . . ."

Thomas laughed. "Perhaps we'll be neighbors, Trooper. Maybe we'll even work together again."

Lincoln winced. "That much I'll have to see about, sir. Somehow I don't think I should include that possibility when I talk to my wife."

Thomas patted the young man on the shoulder. "You do what you have to, Trooper. But I can tell you now, you make one hell of a good Watson. Keep that in mind."

"I will, sir."

"Rest now, Trooper Reeves." Thomas stood up stiffly, trying not to wince at his own pain. He turned back toward the bedroom. "At least for a little while, that's what I'm going to do."

The employees of THORNDIKE PRESS hope you have enjoyed this Large Print book. All our Large Print books are designed for easy reading — and they're made to last.

Other Thorndike Large Print books are available at your library, through selected bookstores, or directly from us. Suggestions for books you would like to see in Large Print are always welcome.

For more information about current and upcoming titles, please call or mail your name and address to:

THORNDIKE PRESS
PO Box 159
Thorndike, Maine 04986
800/223-6121
207/948-2962